THE HEINLE Picture Dictionary BEGINNING WORKBOOK

SECOND EDITION

NATIONAL GEOGRAPHIC LEARNING | HEINLE CENGAGE Learning

Australia • Brazil • Japan • Korea • Mexico • Singapore • Spain • United Kingdom • United States

NATIONAL GEOGRAPHIC LEARNING | HEINLE CENGAGE Learning

The Heinle Picture Dictionary, Beginning Workbook, Second Edition

Publisher: Sherrise Roehr

Senior Development Editor: Jill Korey O'Sullivan

Development Editors: Brenden Layte, Maureen Sotoohi

Director of Global Marketing: Ian Martin

Product Marketing Manager: Lindsey Miller

Director of Content and Media Production: Michael Burggren

Content Project Manager: Mark Rzeszutek

Senior Print Buyer: Mary Beth Hennebury

Compositor: PreMediaGlobal

Cover Design: Michael Rosenquest

Cover Photo: Brian Skerry

Senior Technology Product Manager: Scott Rule

Workbook + Audio CD
ISBN: 978-1-133-56317-4

Workbook
ISBN: 978-1-133-56311-2

National Geographic Learning
20 Channel Center Street
Boston, MA 02210
USA

Cengage Learning is a leading provider of customized learning solutions with office locations around the globe, including Singapore, the United Kingdom, Australia, Mexico, Brazil, and Japan.

Cengage Learning products are represented in Canada by Nelson Education, Ltd.

Visit National Geographic Learning online at: **ngl.cengage.com**
Visit our corporate website at **cengage.com**

Printed in the United States of America
7 8 9 10 11 12 26 25 24 23

Credits

Illustrators

James Edwards/The Beranbaum Group: pp. 65, 123
Bob Kayganich/IllustrationOnLine.com: pp. 4, 24, 50, 162, 194 (1 Across), 194 (8 Down), 226
Cheryl Kirk Noll/CATugeau LLC: pp. 9, 11, 114, 117
Barbara Kiwak/Gwen Walters Artist Representative: p. 29 (A–F)
Greg LaFever/Scott Hull Associates Inc.: pp. 12–13, 76, 80, 153, 156
Mapping Specialists: pp. 44, 174 (bottom)
Precision Graphics: pp. v, 7, 52, 54, 72 (bottom), 85, 96, 133, 145 (bottom A–H), 158, 166, 168, 172, 174 (top), 186, 206
Susan Spellman/Gwen Walters Artist Representative: pp. 5 (1–6 bottom), 94, 101, 105, 113, 132, 151, 160, 188, 204
Carol Stutz Illustration: pp. 57, 120, 124, 127, 131
Gary Torrisi/Gwen Walters Artist Representative: pp. 22, 34, 37, 69, 71, 75
Meryl Treatner/CATugeau LLC: pp. 18, 21, 136–137, 167 (bottom)

Photos

Unit One – Unit Icon Credit: © Tom Grill/Corbis; 2: © Hemera Photo-Objects; 8: © Voronin76/Shutterstock.com, © Mark Payne/Shutterstock.com, © Robynrg/Shutterstock.com; 10: © Hemera Photo-Objects, © Photodisc Green/Getty Images; 14: © Hemera Photo-Objects; 15: © Hemera Photo-Object; 16: © Hemera Photo-Objects, © JNT Visual/Shutterstock.com, © iStockphoto.com/shuchunke, © Oleksiy Mark/Shutterstock.com
Unit Two – Unit Icon Credit: © Royalty-Free/Corbis
Unit Three – Unit Icon Credit: © Thinkstock/Getty Images; 28: © Hemera Photo-Object, © David Young-Wolff/PhotoEdit; 29: © Hemera Photo-Objects; 30: © Hemera Photo-Object, © Damons Point Light/Alamy
Unit Four – Unit Icon Credit: © Jose Luis Pelaez, Inc./Corbis; 32: © Hemera Photo-Objects; 33: © Hemera Photo-Objects; 36: © Hemera Photo-Objects; 38: © Hemera Photo-Objects; 41: © Hemera Photo-Objects, © iStockphoto.com/bo1982
Unit Five – Unit Icon Credit: © Photodisc Collection/Getty Images; 46: © Hemera Photo-Objects, © Stockbyte Platinum/Getty Images; 48: © Hemera Photo-Objects; 58: © Hemera Photo-Objects; 60: © Corbis, © iStockphoto.com/wsmahar, © Jupiter Images, © iStockphoto.com/Rich Legg;
Unit Six – Unit Icon Credit: © Cydney Conger/Flirt/CORBIS, 62: © Hemera Photo-Objects, © iStockphoto.com/JohnnyGreig; 68: © Hemera Photo-Objects, © Brand X Pictures/Fotosearch; 70: © Hemera Photo-Objects; 73: © Hemera Photo-Objects, © Digital Archive Japan/Alamy, © Brand X Pictures/Fotosearch
Unit Seven – Unit Icon Credit: © Burke-Triolo Productions/Getty Images; 82: © Photodisc Collection/Getty Images, © Maks Narodenko/Shutterstock.com, © bergamont/Shutterstock.com, © Roxana Bashyrova/Shutterstock.com, © Keith Seaman/FoodPix, © Lepas/Shutterstock.com, © Hemera Photo-Objects, © bajinda/Shutterstock.com, © Nattika/Shutterstock.com, © Tatiana Popova/Shutterstock.com, © EM Arts/Shutterstock.com, © Dionisvera/Shutterstock.com, © Serhiy Shullye/Shutterstock.com; 85: © Photodisc Collection/Getty Images; 86: © Hemera Photo-Objects; 88: © Digital Archive Japan/Inmagine; 90: © Hemera Photo-Objects, 91: © Hemera Photo-Objects; 92: © Hemera Photo-Objects; 97: © Hemera Photo-Objects; 98: © Hemera Photo-Objects; 100: © Hemera Photo-Objects; 102: © Hemera Photo-Objects
Unit Eight – Unit Icon Credit: © C Squared Studios/Getty Images; 104: © Hemera Photo-Objects; 106: © Hemera Photo-Objects; 108: © Hemera Photo-Objects; 109: © Hemera Photo-Objects; 110: © Hemera Photo-Objects, © Royalty-Free/Corbis; 111: © Hemera Photo-Objects; 112: © Lawrence Manning/Corbis, © C Squared Studios/Photodisc/Getty Images, © Royalty-Free/Corbis, © Photodisc/Fotosearch, © Digital Vision/Getty Images; 116: © Hemera Photo-Objects; 117: © Hemera Photo-Objects
Unit Nine – Unit Icon Credit: © Wes Thompson/Corbis; 129: © Adrian Matthiassen/Shutterstock.com, © Photodisc Green/Getty Images
Unit Ten – Unit Icon Credit: © Herrmann/Starke/Corbis; 138: © Hemera Photo-Objects, © Creatas/Fotosearch; 140: © Hemera Photo-Objects; 141: © Hemera Photo-Objects; 142: © Hemera Photo-Objects, © Lawrence Manning/Corbis
Unit Eleven – Unit Icon Credit: © PictureNet/Corbis; 146: © Hemera Photo-Objects, © Vtls/Shutterstock.com; 148: © Hemera Photo-Objects; 152: © Hemera Photo Objects; 155: Hemera Photo Objects; 161: © Comstock Images/Getty Images, © Hemera Photo Objects, © John Coletti; 163: © iStockphoto.com/miflippo, © John Coletti, © Coprid/Shutterstock.com, © Jules Frazier/Photodisc/Getty Images, © Hemera Photo Objects; 164: © Hemera Photo Objects
Unit Twelve – Unit Icon Credit: © L. Clarke/Corbis; 170: © Hemera Photo Objects, © Igumnova Irina/Shutterstock.com, © Konstantin Mironov/Shutterstock.com; 174: © thumb/Shutterstock.com; 176: © Digital Vision/Getty Images, © Comstock/Fotosearch, © Courtesy of NASA, © Paul Fleet/Shutterstock.com, © Vasily Smirnov/Shutterstock.com, © Photodisc Red/Getty Images
Unit Thirteen – Unit Icon Credit: © Digital Vision/Getty Images; 178: © Hemera Photo Objects; 180: © Hemera Photo Objects; 182: © Hemera Photo Objects; 184: © Hemera Photo Objects; 187: Hemera Photo Objects, © Tom Brakefield/Digital Vision/Getty Images; 188: © Hemera Photo Objects; 190: © Hemera Photo Objects
Unit Fourteen – Unit Icon Credit: © Don Farrall/Getty Images; 192: © Hemera Photo-Objects; 198: © Brand X Pictures/Fotosearch, © Fuse/Getty Images, © James Steidl/Shutterstock.com, © Jason and Bonnie Grower/Shutterstock.com, © Stephen Coburn/Shutterstock.com, © Royalty- Free/Corbis; 200: © Photodisc Green/Getty Images, © Brand X Pictures/Getty Images
Unit Fifteen - Unit Icon Credit: © Don Farrall/Getty Images; 202: © Hemera Photo-Objects, © Royalty-Free/Corbis; 203: © Hemera Photo-Objects; 208: © Hemera Photo-Objects
Unit Sixteen - Unit Icon Credit: © Digital Vision/Getty Images; 210: © Hemera Photo-Objects; 213: © Hemera Photo-Objects; 214: © Hemera Photo-Objects; 216: © Hemera Photo- Objects, © TaurusPhotography/Alamy, © Vitalii Nesterchuk/Shutterstock.com; 218: © Hemera Photo-Objects; 220: © Hemera Photo-Objects; 222: © Hemera Photo-Objects; 223: © Hemera Photo-Objects; 224: © Hemera Photo-Objects; 228: © Hemera Photo-Objects

To the Teacher

The Heinle Picture Dictionary Beginning Workbook, 2nd edition provides students with a variety of activities to practice and reinforce the vocabulary learned in *The Heinle Picture Dictionary.* The workbook can be used in conjunction with class instruction or can be used on its own. This edition of the workbook features new activities, audio, and art to go with the updated word lists presented in *The Heinle Picture Dictionary, 2nd edition.*

The workbook follows the same page-by-page format as *The Heinle Picture Dictionary.* For example, after introducing a spread such as City Square (pages 58–59) in the dictionary, students can complete the corresponding pages in the workbook (pages 58–59). The exercises can be done in class, in small groups, or assigned as homework.

The workbook lessons follow a general pattern. The first exercise is often illustrated and asks students to identify specific vocabulary items. A variety of exercises follows. Students are asked to look in their dictionaries and answer *true / false* statements, to count the number of people or items they see, or to match sentences to the actions in the dictionary. In other activities, students group words into categories, complete sentences, match words, or put steps in order. Students will also enjoy traditional "fun" vocabulary exercises, such as crossword puzzles, word searches, and scrambled words. The final activity often asks students to complete sentences with information about their own lives and interests.

A unique and important feature of this workbook is the listening activity that appears in each lesson. The listening activities reinforce the vocabulary in a number of ways. Some ask students to recognize the words in sentences or short dialogues about the topic. While listening, students may identify pictures, circle or write the vocabulary word they hear, complete a checklist, decide if statements are true or false, or follow a map. In several activities, students are asked to choose the sound they hear, such as a musical instrument, a sport, or an animal. There is ample support for the listening exercises, with pictures and word boxes providing spelling and word clues. It will be necessary to pause between each item in an exercise to allow students sufficient time to choose the correct answer. Students often find it helpful to listen to the exercises more than once. When the listening activity is done in class, students should be encouraged to listen to the CD again at home for review.

The final page of each workbook unit provides a *Word Study* box. These are strategies for vocabulary learning. Learners need several exposures to a new word or phrase in order to learn it. Short practice periods with frequent review are usually more effective than long study sessions. Teachers can introduce the strategies at any time and in any order. Allow class time in which to discuss the ideas and get student feedback. Some students may have additional helpful strategies to offer the class. Students should identify two or three strategies that are effective for them. Time spent in class reflecting on how to study can help students acquire more effective learning strategies.

Along with these features, the 2nd edition of the workbooks include the *Grammar Connection* where the content of each lesson is used to teach or review an appropriate grammar point. A grammar point is presented, along with notes on its usage, before students get a chance to practice it using words from *The Heinle Picture Dictionary.*

Many students find that a personal vocabulary notebook helps them record new words and allows for quick review sessions. A sample page from such a notebook and additional suggestions for choosing and recording new words are presented on the next page.

Enjoy using *The Heinle Picture Dictionary Workbook* in your class and watching your students' vocabulary grow!

A Vocabulary Notebook

Many students find that a vocabulary notebook is a helpful way to learn and review new vocabulary words. The sample below shows part of a potential vocabulary notebook page.

What words should I put in my vocabulary notebook?

This is *your* personal notebook. Put in words *you* want to remember. Write some new words from your dictionary. Add words that you see or hear in school or at work. Write words that you hear on TV or in a song you like.

How should I write the words?

Students write new words in different ways. Sometimes, you will remember the word when you see it. For other words, you can translate the word into your own language or draw a simple picture. You may also want to write a short sentence with the word or write a definition.

How can I learn new words?

There are three rules for learning new vocabulary:

Rule #1: Review.
Rule #2: Review.
Rule #3: Review again.

Contents

1 Basic Words

2 School

3 Family

4 People

5 Community

6 Housing

7 Food

8 Clothing

9 Transportation

10 Health

11 Work

12 Earth and Space

13 Animals, Plants, and Habitats

14 School Subjects

15 The Arts

16 Recreation

Numbers

A Write the missing number.

1. one, ___two___, three, four
2. three, ________, five, six
3. six, ________, eight, nine
4. ten, eleven, ________, thirteen
5. eleven, twelve, ________, fourteen
6. fifteen, sixteen, ________, eighteen
7. eighteen, nineteen, twenty, ________

B Write the number of dots.

a. ___nine___ b. ________ c. ________ d. ________

e. ________ f. ________ g. ________ h. ________

C Match the number and the word.

5	a. 18	1. seventeen
____	b. 80	2. fifty
____	c. 17	3. sixteen
____	d. 16	4. seventy
____	e. 50	5. eighteen
____	f. 60	6. eighty
____	g. 70	7. sixty

Grammar Connection: Singular and Plural Nouns

Singular Nouns	Plural Nouns	
a book	books	five books
a car	cars	two cars

Note:
- *Singular* means one.
- *Plural* means more than one.
- Add *s* to the end of most nouns to make them plural.

D Write the plural form.

1. a boy ten boys
2. a girl two ____________
3. a number five ____________
4. a school two ____________
5. a house four ____________
6. a student twenty ____________
7. a dollar ten ____________
8. a pencil three ____________

E Complete with information about yourself.

1. My address is ____.
2. My phone number is ____.
3. My school has ____________________ floors.
4. My classroom is on the ____________________ floor.
5. My class is in Room ____________________.

CD 1
Track 1

F Listen and write the floor and the room number.

1. Mr. Aker's office is on the fourth floor in Room 7.
2. Mrs. Brown's office is on the ____________ floor in Room ____________.
3. Dr. Chin's office is on the ____________ floor in Room ____________.
4. Mr. Dean's office is on the ____________ floor in Room ____________.
5. Mr. Edgar's office is on the ____________ floor in Room ____________.
6. Mrs. Franco's office is on the ____________ floor in Room ____________.

Time

A Match.

__b__ **1.** a minute **a.** 2011 to 2020

____ **2.** an hour **b.** 3:07 to 3:08

____ **3.** a day **c.** Tuesday

____ **4.** a month **d.** 3:00 to 4:00

____ **5.** a year **e.** January

____ **6.** a decade **f.** 2017

B Show the times on the clocks.

1. four o'clock

2. twelve o'clock

3. four-thirty

4. seven fifteen

5. three forty-five

6. eight-oh-five

7. twelve twenty

8. two fifty-five

C Put the time words in order.

1. ____morning____

2. ______________

3. ______________

4. ______________

5. ______________

6. ______________

noon
~~morning~~
night
evening
afternoon
midnight

Grammar Connection: Prepositions of Time - *at / in*

at	at	in
at 1:00 **at** 4:30 **at** 11:45	**at** noon **at** night **at** midnight	**in the** morning **in the** afternoon **in the** evening

D Complete with the correct preposition.

1. I get up early ___in___ the morning.
2. I eat breakfast ____________ 7:00.
3. I go to school ____________ the morning.
4. I eat lunch ____________ noon.
5. I do my homework ____________ the afternoon.
6. I work ____________ the evening.
7. I get home ____________ midnight.
8. I go to bed ____________ 1:00.

CD 1
Track 2

E Listen to Henry's schedule. Write the time under each picture.

1. ___*7:00*___

2. ____________

3. ____________

4. ____________

5. ____________

6. ____________

F Complete with information about your schedule.

1. I get up at ____________.
2. I eat breakfast at ____________.
3. I leave the house at ____________.
4. I get to work/school at ____________.
5. I get home at ____________.
6. I go to bed at ____________.

Calendar

A Write the missing days.

Sunday, ____________________, Tuesday, ____________________,

Thursday, Friday, ____________________

B Complete the sentences. Write the day(s).

1. Today is ____________________.
2. Yesterday was ____________________.
3. Tomorrow is ____________________.
4. The weekdays are ____________________, ____________________,

   ____________________, ____________________, and ____________________.
5. The weekend days are ____________________ and ____________________.
6. I go to school on ____.
7. I work on ____.

C Write the missing months.

January, ____________________, March, ____________________, May,

June, ____________________, ____________________, September,

____________________, ____________________, December

D Complete the sentences. Write the month.

1. It is ____________________.
2. Last month was ____________________.
3. Next month is ____________________.
4. My birthday is in ____________________.
5. My favorite holiday is in ____________________.

Grammar Connection: Prepositions of Time - *on* / *at*

on	at
on Sunday **on** Friday	**at** 9:00 **at** 12:00

Note:

- Use *on* for days of the week.
- Use *at* for exact time.

E **Look at Mario's calendar. Complete the sentences with the correct day and preposition.**

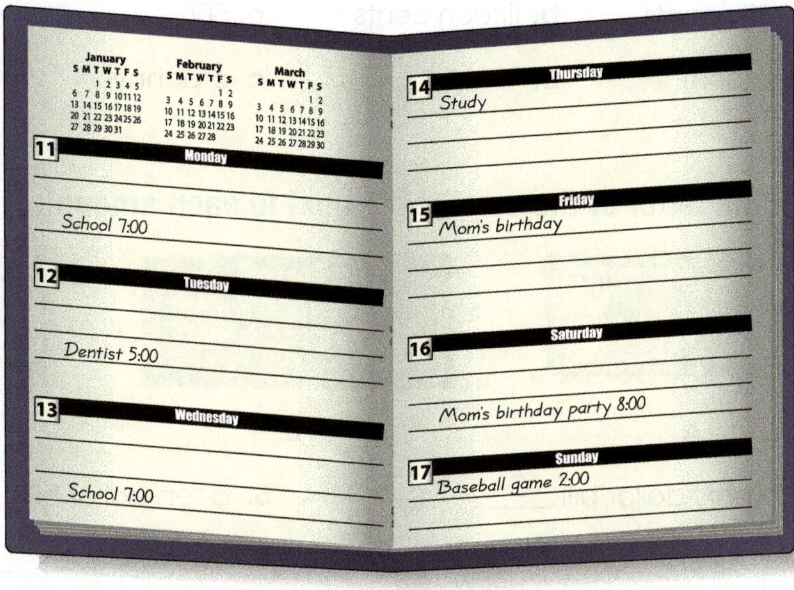

1. Mario has a dentist appointment ______on Tuesday at 5:00______.
2. Mario will study ____________________.
3. Mario has a baseball game ____________________.
4. His mother's birthday is ____________________.
5. The party for his mother is ____________________.
6. Mario has school ____________________.

CD 1 Track 3

F **Listen and write the day you hear.**

1. ___Wednesday___	6. ______________
2. ______________	7. ______________
3. ______________	8. ______________
4. ______________	9. ______________
5. ______________	10. ______________

Money and Shopping

A Circle the three amounts that are the same.

1. **a.** 5¢ **b.** five cents **c.** fifty cents **d.** a nickel
2. **a.** a dime **b.** a nickel **c.** 10¢ **d.** ten cents
3. **a.** a dollar **b.** $1.00 **c.** one dollar **d.** $10.00
4. **a.** 25¢ **b.** a quarter **c.** 50¢ **d.** twenty-five cents
5. **a.** fifty cents **b.** fifteen cents **c.** 50¢ **d.** a half dollar
6. **a.** a cent **b.** 1¢ **c.** a penny **d.** 10¢

B Write the letter of the correct bill next to each amount.

A

B

C

1. a twenty-dollar bill _C_
2. five dollars ____
3. $20 ____
4. $5 ____
5. a ten-dollar bill ____
6. twenty dollars ____
7. a five-dollar bill ____
8. ten dollars ____

C Circle the larger amount.

1. **a.** a quarter **b.** a half dollar
2. **a.** a dime **b.** a nickel
3. **a.** ten cents **b.** a penny
4. **a.** a half dollar **b.** a dollar
5. **a.** a nickel **b.** a quarter
6. **a.** ten dollars **b.** twenty dollars
7. **a.** a quarter **b.** a dime
8. **a.** twenty-five cents **b.** fifty cents

CD 1
Track 4

D Listen and write the amount. Use *¢* or *$*.

a. 25¢   d. ________   g. ________

b. ________   e. ________   h. ________

c. ________   f. ________   i. ________

Grammar Connection: *How much* Questions

How much	is	this book?
How much	are	these books?

It is $15.00.
They are $15.00 each.

Note:
- Use *is* with a singular noun.
- Use *are* with a plural noun.

E Complete the questions.

1. How much ___are___ these pencils? They are $1.00 each.
2. How much ________ this dictionary? It is $12.00.
3. How much ________ these flowers? They are $8.00.
4. How much ________ these shoes? They are $35.00.
5. How much ________ hat? It is $14.00.
6. How much ________ pens? They are $3.00 each.

F Complete the conversation.

cash	sale price	sales tax
credit cards	~~regular price~~	

Shopper: How much is this shirt?

Cashier: The (1) ___regular price___ is $32, but it's on sale. The (2) ________ is $25.

Shopper: Is there (3) ________?

Cashier: Yes, the sales tax is 5%.

Shopper: Can I use a personal check?

Cashier: No, we only take (4) ________ or (5) ________.

Colors

A Unscramble each word. Write the color.

1. llyeow ___yellow___
2. uble ____________
3. kinp ____________
4. clabk ____________
5. uppelr ____________
6. oreang ____________
7. ayrg ____________
8. voryi ____________
9. sirlev ____________
10. neerg ____________

B Write the color word.

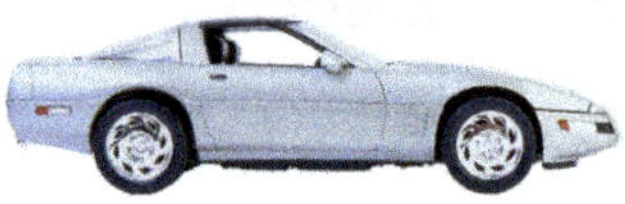

1. a ___silver___ car

2. a ____________ bird

3. a ____________ pen

4. a ____________ ring

5. a ____________ chair

6. a ____________ flower

7. a(n) ____________ cup

8. a ____________ tie

9. a ____________ ball

CD 1
Track 5

C Listen and write the number of each conversation under the correct picture.

a. ____________

b. ____________

c. ____________

d. ____________

e. ____________

f. ____1____

g. ____________

h. ____________

Grammar Connection: Singular and Plural *be*

What color	**is**	your **pencil**?
What color	**are**	your **pencils**?

It	**is**	yellow.
They	**are**	yellow.

D Complete the answers with *is* or *are*.

1. What color is his cap? It is ____red____ .
2. What color is his hair? It ____________ black.
3. What color is his shirt? It ____________ yellow.
4. What color is his backpack? It ____________ green.
5. What color are his pants? They ____________ blue.
6. What color are his shoes? They ____________ white.

E Answer the questions.

1. What color are your eyes? They are ____________.
2. What color is your hair? It is ____________.
3. What color is your book? ____________.
4. What color is your pencil? ____________.
5. What color are your shoes? ____________.

In, On, Under

A **Complete the sentences with the correct preposition.**

1. The red box is ___between___ the green box and the yellow box.
2. The white box is ______________ the black box.
3. The black cat is ______________ the white box.
4. The white cat is ______________ the green box.
5. The yellow box is ______________ the black box.
6. The orange cat is ______________ the black box.
7. The red box is ______________ the green box.
8. The white box is ______________ the green box.
9. The pink box is ______________ the other boxes.

behind
on
far from
to the right of
in front of
in
under
to the left of
~~between~~

B **Look at the picture. Circle *T* if the statement is true. Circle *F* if the statement is false.**

1. Adam is on the right of Will. T (F)
2. Will is between Adam and Carlos. T F
3. Will is next to Tran. T F
4. Carlos is on the left of Tran. T F
5. Carlos is between Adam and Will. T F
6. Tran is on the right of Carlos. T F

Grammar Connection: *Where* Questions with *be*

Where	is	the **pencil**?
Where	are	the **pencils**?

It's	on the desk.
They're	on the desk.

Note:

- *It's* is the contraction for *It is*.
- *They're* is the contraction for *They are*.

C Complete the questions with *is* or *are*. Then, match the questions and answers.

f 1. Where is the computer?		a. They're under the table.
___ 2. Where ___ the pencils?		b. It's to the right of the computer.
___ 3. Where ___ the kittens?		c. They're to the left of the computer.
___ 4. Where ___ the cell phone?		d. It's under the table.
___ 5. Where ___ the books?		e. They're on top of the books.
___ 6. Where ___ the pieces of paper?		f. It's on the desk.
___ 7. Where ___ backpack?		g. They're to the right of the computer.

D Listen and write the number of each sentence under the correct picture.

CD 1
Track 6

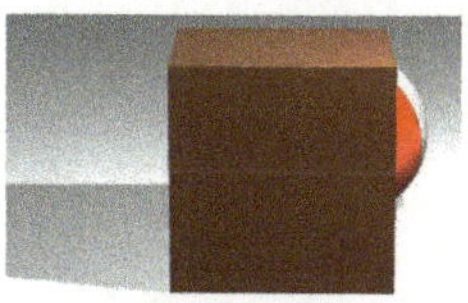

a. ___

b. ___

c. 1

d. ___

e. ___

f. ___

g. ___

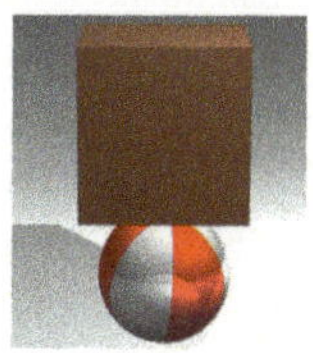

h. ___

Opposites

A Circle the correct word.

1. The box is [open closed].
2. The box is [large small].
3. The box is [full empty].
4. The book is [old new].
5. The book is [clean dirty].
6. The book is [open closed].

B Write the opposite.

1. beautiful ugly
2. strong ______
3. heavy ______
4. dead ______
5. short ______
6. soft ______
7. full ______
8. slow ______
9. thin ______
10. poor ______
11. hot ______
12. open ______

C Look at the opposites in your dictionary. Complete the sentences.

1. He is not short. He is tall.
2. This watch isn't cheap. It's very ______.
3. English isn't easy. It's ______.
4. My baby sister isn't quiet. She's ______.
5. She drives an old car. She doesn't drive a ______ car.
6. China isn't a small country. It's a ______ country.
7. Your shoes aren't clean. They're ______.
8. The windows aren't open. They're ______.

CD 1
Track 7

D Listen to the questions. Circle *Yes* or *No.*

   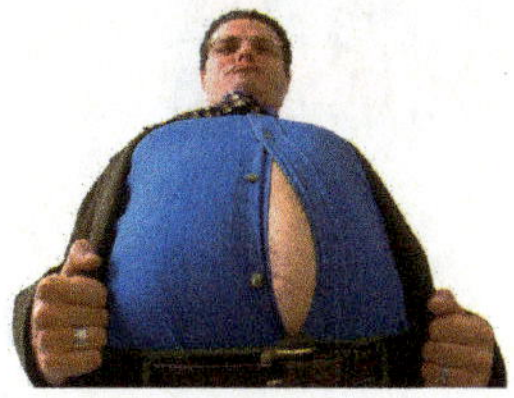

1. Yes No **2.** Yes No **3.** Yes No **4.** Yes No

5. Yes No **6.** Yes No **7.** Yes No **8.** Yes No

Grammar Connection: *Yes / No* Questions and Answers with *be*

Yes / No **Question**	**Affirmative Answer**	**Negative Answer**
Are you old?	**Yes, I am.**	**No, I'm not.**
Is he tall?	**Yes, he is.**	**No, he isn't.**
Is she tall?	**Yes, she is.**	**No, she isn't.**
Is it tall?	**Yes, it is.**	**No, it isn't.**
Are they short?	**Yes, they are.**	**No, they aren't.**

Note:

- Do not contract the affirmative short answers. Yes, he is. NOT: ~~Yes, he's.~~

E Circle the answer to the questions.

1.	Are you young?	Yes, I am.	No, I'm not.
2.	Are you strong?	Yes, I am.	No, I'm not.
3.	Are you cold?	Yes, I am.	No, I'm not.
4.	Are your hands clean?	Yes, they are.	No, they aren't.
5.	Is your school large?	Yes, they are.	No, they aren't.
6.	Is your school old?	Yes, it is.	No, it isn't.
7.	Are the windows open?	Yes, they are.	No, they aren't.
8.	Are the students noisy?	Yes, they are.	No, they aren't.
9.	Is your teacher short?	Yes, he/she is.	No, he/she isn't.
10.	Is English difficult?	Yes, it is.	No, it isn't.

The Telephone

A Write the word for each item.

a charger	a phone number	a calling card
a headset	a cordless phone	~~a smartphone~~

1. a smartphone

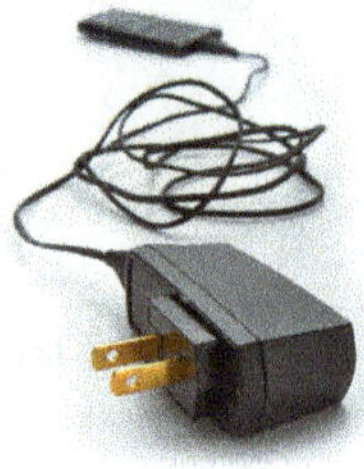

2. ____________

3. ____________

4. ____________

5. ____________

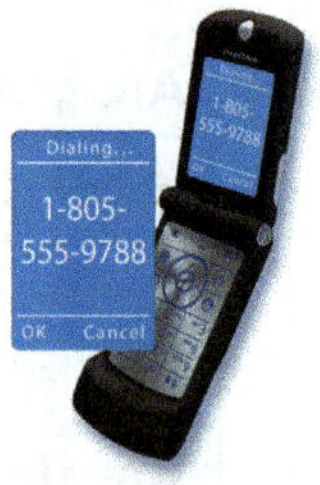

6. ____________

B Circle the correct word.

1. Dial 911 for [emergency assistance information].
2. A(n) [operator caller] gives directory assistance.
3. You can check e-mail on a [smart phone cordless phone].
4. This phone uses a [touchscreen calling card] instead of buttons.
5. This new [app operator] lets me play games on my phone.
6. I use a [caller headset] in my car.
7. My [telephone number receiver] is 555 - 4539.
8. My [time zone area code] is 201.

Grammar Connection: Making a Phone Call

Hi. **This is** Lani Gibson. May I please speak with Tony?

Note:
- When you speak on the phone, introduce yourself with "This is (your name)."

C Complete the sentences. Give your name. Who do you want to speak with?

Hi. This is ____________________.

May I please speak with ____________________?

D Listen to each question. What is each person asking about?

CD 1
Track 8

1. *emergency assistance*
2. ____________________
3. ____________________
4. ____________________
5. ____________________

area code
phone number
time zone
information
~~emergency assistance~~

E Circle the information about yourself.

1. Do you have a cell phone?	Yes, I do.	No, I don't.
2. Do you ever use a phone card?	Yes, I do.	No, I don't.
3. Do you use a headset?	Yes, I do.	No, I don't.
4. Do you ever make international calls?	Yes, I do.	No, I don't.

Word Study

It is difficult to study vocabulary for a long time. Plan to study vocabulary words frequently for short periods of time throughout the day.

Classroom

A Circle the items that are in your classroom.

a clock	an overhead projector	a table	a blackboard
a map	a bulletin board	a desk	a whiteboard
a flag	a bookshelf	a chair	a globe

B Write the word for each item that is on the desk.

test	~~pen~~	notebook
eraser	textbook	pencil

1. ___pen___
2. ______________
3. ______________
4. ______________
5. ______________
6. ______________

C Look at the classroom in your dictionary. Complete these sentences.

textbook	map	~~homework assignment~~	globe
desk	test	bulletin board	poster

1. The teacher is writing the ___homework assignment___ on the board.
2. There is a ______________ to the left of the blackboard.
3. The ______________ is on top of the bookshelf.
4. There are two piles of paper on the teacher's ______________.
5. The ______________ says "Read."
6. One student has a blue ______________ on his desk.
7. One student got an A+ on his ______________.
8. There are flags and pictures on the ______________.

Grammar Connection: Singular and Plural Nouns

Singular	Plural
a chair	chairs
a pencil	pencils

Note:

- *Singular* means one.
- *Plural* means more than one.
- To form the plural of most singular nouns, add *–s* to the noun.

D Write the nouns in the plural form.

1. a clock clocks
2. a desk ________
3. a flag ________
4. a globe ________
5. a map ________
6. a poster ________
7. a table ________
8. a teacher ________
9. a pen ________
10. a book ________

CD 1
Track 9

E Look at the classroom in your dictionary. Listen and circle the correct answer.

1. **(a.)** It's over the bulletin board. **b.** It's next to the overhead projector.
2. **a.** It's on the whiteboard. **b.** It's on the desk.
3. **a.** It's in front of the whiteboard. **b.** It's under the poster.
4. **a.** She's in front of the class. **b.** She's next to the map.
5. **a.** It's under the clock. **b.** It's next to the blackboard.
6. **a.** It's on the table. **b.** It's on the bookshelf.
7. **a.** It's next to the globe. **b.** It's over the whiteboard.
8. **a.** It's on the board. **b.** It's on the desk.
9. **a.** They're in the classroom. **b.** They're at home.

F Write six items you bring to class every day.

1. ________
2. ________
3. ________
4. ________
5. ________
6. ________

Listen, Read, Write

A Check the things you do in your classroom.

____ **1.** We listen to the teacher.

____ **2.** We share books.

____ **3.** We discuss our ideas.

____ **4.** We copy sentences.

____ **5.** We look up new words.

____ **6.** We go to the board.

____ **7.** We read books.

____ **8.** We take a break.

B Circle the correct word.

1. Copy the [(sentence) board].

2. Hand in your [paper name].

3. Look up a [book word].

4. Raise your [word hand].

5. Erase the [book board].

6. Collect the [papers sentences].

7. Share a [book names].

8. Close your [word book].

9. Write your [name group].

10. Take a(n) [idea break].

C Follow the directions.

1. Check the correct answer.

5 + 6 = _✓_ 11 ____ 12 ____ 13

2. Underline the correct answer.

9 + 7 = 14 15 16

3. Darken the correct oval.

6 + 7 = ○ 12 ○ 13 ○ 14

4. Cross out the wrong answers.

7 + 8 = 15 16 17

5. Circle the correct answer.

9 + 9 = 16 17 18

6. Fill in the blank.

4 + 5 = ____

7. Match the items.

6	eight
7	seven
8	six

8. Correct the mistake.

6 + 6 = 11

CD 1
Track 10

D Listen to each sentence. Write the number of the sentence under the correct picture.

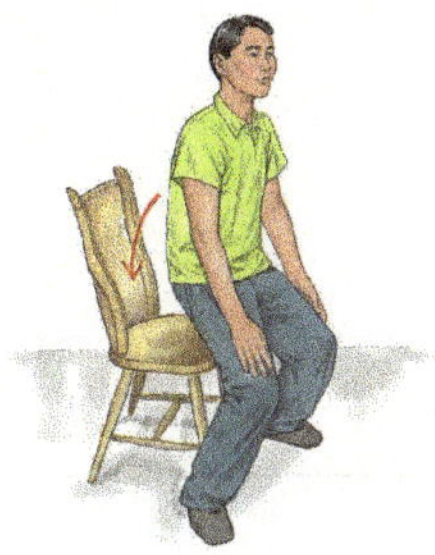

a. ________

b. ________

c. ________

d. ________

e. ________

f. ________

g. ___1___

h. ________

Grammar Connection: Classroom Instructions

Go to the board.	**Write** your name.

E Complete the sentences with the correct word.

Open	Circle	Erase	Raise	Copy

1. ___*Circle*___ the correct answer.
2. ________ your books.
3. ________ your hand.
4. ________ the sentences.
5. ________ board.

Look up	Take	Spell	Correct	Hand out

6. ________ a break.
7. ________ the mistake.
8. ________ the papers.
9. ________ your name.
10. ________ the word in the dictionary.

School

A Where is each student?

cafeteria | auditorium | language lab | gym | classroom | ~~library~~

1. She is in the library.

2. He is in the ______.

3. She is in the ______.

4. She is in the ______.

5. He is in the ______.

6. He is in the ______.

B Complete the sentences.

water fountain	~~gym~~	teachers' lounge	report cards
library	cafeteria	school nurse	backpacks

1. Students play sports in the gym.
2. Students get a drink of water at the ______.
3. Students go to the ______ when they feel sick.
4. Students can study quietly in the ______.
5. Students eat lunch in the ______.
6. Students carry their books in their ______.
7. The teachers eat and relax in the ______.
8. Students receive their grades on their ______.

Grammar Connection: *There is / There are*

There is	one student in the classroom.
There are	ten students in the classroom.

Note:

- A sentence beginning with *There is* or *There are* often tells how many.
- Use *There is* with a singular subject.
- Use *There are* with a plural subject.

C Complete the sentences with *There is* or *There are.*

1. ____There are____ four students in the library.
2. ________________ three students in the language lab.
3. ________________ one student in the guidance counselor's office.
4. ________________ six students in the classroom.
5. ________________ one student in the nurse's office.
6. ________________ four students in the library.
7. ________________ six students in the cafeteria.
8. ________________ one student in front of the lockers.

CD 1
Track 11

D Listen to this student talk about his school. Match each room number with the correct room or person.

__g__	**1.** Room 101	**a.** classroom
____	**2.** Room 104	**b.** library
____	**3.** Room 120	**c.** guidance counselor
____	**4.** Room 202	**d.** language lab
____	**5.** Room 206	**e.** nurse
____	**6.** Room 209	**f.** cafeteria
____	**7.** Room 215	**g.** principal
____	**8.** Room 301	**h.** teachers' lounge

E Which of these do you have in your school? Make a check next to each item.

____ language lab	____ gym	____ teachers' lounge
____ nurse	____ auditorium	____ cafeteria
____ water fountain	____ library	____ lockers

Computers

A Write the word for each computer item.

CD-ROM	key	USB port	keyboard
flash drive	~~screen~~	laptop computer	trackpad

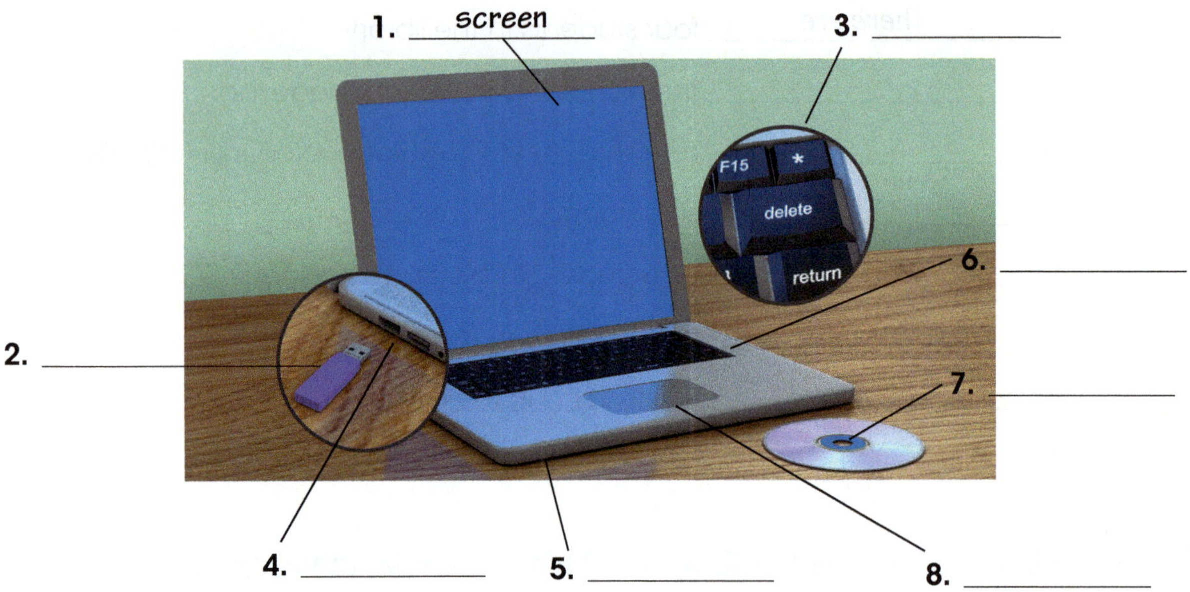

B Unscramble each computer word.

1. soume mouse
2. obtlora ____________
3. caleb ____________
4. life ____________
5. coin ____________
6. yek ____________
7. muen ____________
8. creens ____________

Grammar Connection: Simple Present Tense with *I*

I	have need want	a printer.

I	don't have don't need don't want	a printer.

C Complete these sentences about your computer equipment with *have*, *need*, or *want*.

1. I want a tablet.
2. ________ a laptop computer.
3. ________ a printer.
4. ________ a scanner.
5. ________ a flash drive.
6. ________ a projector.
7. ________ a power strip.
8. ________ a desktop computer.

CD 1
Track 12

D Listen to the sentences. Write the word you hear.

projector	key	laptop	icon
printer	CD-ROM	~~scanner~~	e-mail

1. I am using a scanner.
2. He has a ________.
3. The ________ is on the table.
4. Send me an ________.
5. Press the *Enter* ________.
6. Click on that ________.
7. Put the ________ in the computer.
8. There is paper in the ________.

E Check the things you can do.

- ☐ 1. I can send an e-mail message.
- ☐ 2. I can use the Internet.
- ☐ 3. I can use a flash drive.
- ☐ 4. I can use a printer.
- ☐ 5. I can scan a picture.
- ☐ 6. I can remember my passwords!

Word Study

There are many words on each page of your dictionary. You know some of the words already. Circle the words that are new for you. When you open your book, study these words first.

Family

A **Write each family member under *Male* or *Female*.**

~~grandfather~~	father	aunt	grandmother
sister	uncle	son	brother
mother	husband	daughter	wife

Male		Female	
grandfather	________	________	________
________	________	________	________
________	________	________	________

Grammar Connection: Possessive Nouns

Martin is **Claudia's** husband.
Erik is **Claudia's** son.
Erik is **Claudia and Martin's** son.

Note:
- Use *'s* with nouns to show possession.
- When there are two nouns, add *'s* to the second noun.

B **What are the relationships between the people in this family? Complete each sentence with a possessive noun. Some sentences have two correct answers.**

1. Erik is Kayla's brother.
2. Kayla is __________ daughter.
3. Martin is __________ father.
4. Claudia is __________ mother.
5. Claudia is __________ wife.
6. Kayla is __________ sister.
7. Erik is __________ son.
8. Martin is __________ husband.

C **Complete the sentences with the correct relationships between the people in this family.**

Bess: Hi. I'm Bess. Jim is my (1)___husband___. I have two children. Mary is my (2)__________ and Ed is my (3)__________. I have four (4)__________. Sarah is my (5)__________.

Mary: Hi. I'm Mary. Larry is my (6)__________. Ed is my (7)__________ and Sarah is my (8)__________. Tony and Tommy are my (9)__________.

Jacob: Hi. I'm Jacob. Larry and Mary are my (10)__________. Jim and Bess are my (11)__________. Ed is my (12)__________ and Sarah is my (13)__________. Tony and Tommy are my (14)__________.

CD 1
Track 13

D **Look at the family in Exercise C and listen to the questions. Circle the correct answers.**

1. (**a.**) Bess	**b.** Mary	**6. a.** Sarah	**b.** Tony
2. a. Larry	**b.** Ed	**7. a.** Jacob	**b.** Jim
3. a. Emma	**b.** Bess	**8. a.** Bess	**b.** Sarah
4. a. Jim	**b.** Ed	**9. a.** Tony	**b.** Ed
5. a. Tony	**b.** Emma	**10. a.** Jacob	**b.** Emma

Raising a Child

A **Match each sentence with the correct picture.**

1. A mother is rocking her child. __B__
2. A baby is crawling. ____
3. A mother is nursing her child. ____
4. A mother is dressing her child. ____
5. A mother is bathing her child. ____
6. A baby is crying. ____

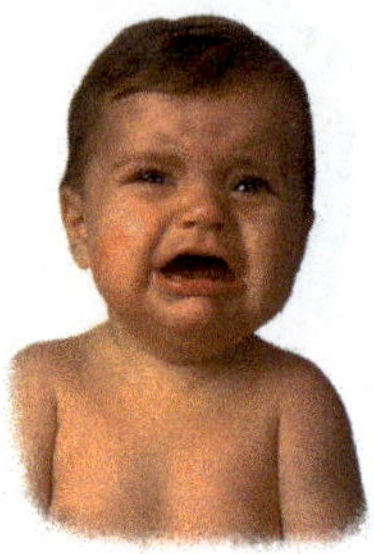

A

B

C

D

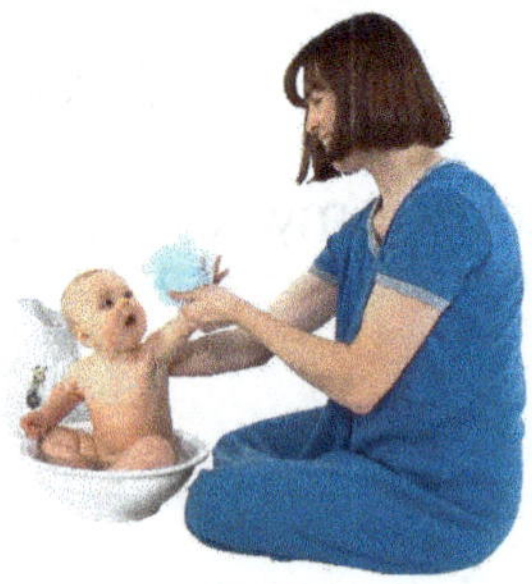

E

F

B **A mother is talking to her young child. Match what she is saying and what she is doing.**

__g__ **1.** "Good girl!"

____ **2.** "This is a story about three bears."

____ **3.** "Let's take out your toy car."

____ **4.** "Let's put your shoes on."

____ **5.** "Let's put your seat belt on."

____ **6.** "Good night, my little girl."

____ **7.** "Go to your room!"

a. The mother is reading to her child.

b. The mother is dressing her child.

c. The mother is protecting her child.

d. The mother is putting her child to bed.

e. The mother is disciplining her child.

f. The mother is playing with her child.

g. The mother is praising her child.

Grammar Connection: Polite Requests

Please hold	the baby.
Please play	with the baby.

Note:

- Begin a polite request with *Please*.
- Use the base form of the verb in a polite request.

C Write each sentence under the correct picture.

Please feed the baby.	Please bathe the baby.
Please dress the baby.	~~Please change the baby.~~

1. Please change the baby.

3. ____________________

2. ____________________

4. ____________________

CD 1
Track 14

D Listen to each sentence. Write the number of each sentence under the correct picture.

a. ____________________

b. ____________________

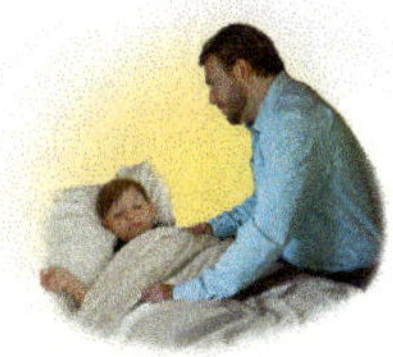

c. ____________________

d. ____________________

e. 1

f. ____________________

Life Events

A **Write the phrase for each event.**

raise a family	become grandparents	have a baby
be pregnant	get married	graduate
get engaged	~~buy a house~~	celebrate a birthday

1. buy a house

2. ____________________

3. ____________________

4. ____________________

5. ____________________

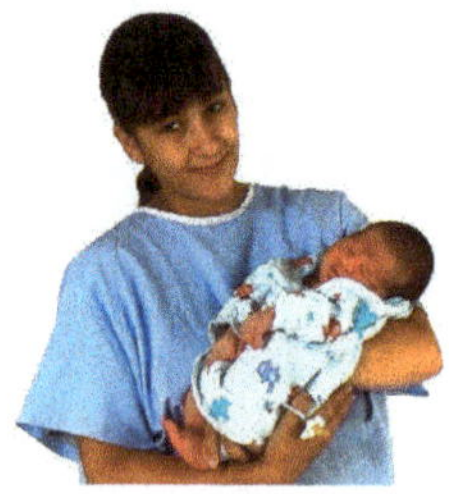

6. ____________________

7. ____________________

8. ____________________

9. ____________________

B **Look at the pictures of the life events in your dictionary. Write the number of the correct event after each sentence.**

1. She is going to college. 6
2. She is raising a family. ____
3. She is retiring. ____
4. She is immigrating. ____
5. She is getting engaged. ____
6. She is getting a job. ____
7. She is taking a vacation. ____
8. She is learning to walk. ____

Grammar Connection: *I would like to*

I would like to	travel to Paris.
I would like to	go to college.

Note:
- *I would like to* describes something that you want to do.
- Use the base form of the verb after *I would like to.*

D What would you like to do in the future? Complete the sentences.

1. Next year, I would like to ____________________.
2. In two years, I would like to ____________________.
3. In three years, I would like to ____________________.
4. In five years, ____________________.
5. In ten years, ____________________.
6. Sometime in the future, ____________________.

CD 1 Track 15

E Listen to the life of John Lennon. Match the dates and the events.

d	1. 1940	a.	He starts the Beatles with three friends.
____	2. 1961	b.	He and his wife have a baby, Julian.
____	3. 1962	c.	He and Cynthia Powell get divorced.
____	4. 1963	d.	John Lennon is born.
____	5. 1964	e.	He plays with the Beatles for the last time.
____	6. 1968	f.	He dies in New York.
____	7. 1969	g.	He and Cynthia Powell get married.
____	8. 1969	h.	The Beatles travel to the United States.
____	9. 1975	i.	He and Yoko have a baby, Sean.
____	10. 1980	j.	He marries Yoko Ono.

Word Study

Cover the word list. Look at the pictures. Say the word or phrase for each picture as you uncover the word list. Put a ✓ next to the words you need to study.

Face and Hair

A Add two words to each category.

~~long~~	~~curly~~	straight	shoulder-length
~~a bun~~	cornrows	short	pigtails
~~brown~~	wavy	blond	black

Hair Color	Hair Length	Hair Type	Hair Style
brown	long	curly	a bun

B Cross out the word that does not belong.

1. **a.** short **b.** long **c.** ~~braids~~ **d.** shoulder-length
2. **a.** blond **b.** brown **c.** red **d.** a ponytail
3. **a.** a mole **b.** braids **c.** freckles **d.** a dimple
4. **a.** red **b.** wavy **c.** straight **d.** curly
5. **a.** a beard **b.** glasses **c.** sideburns **d.** a moustache
6. **a.** pigtails **b.** wavy **c.** cornrows **d.** braids

CD 1
Track 16

C Listen and write the letter of the correct man.

A

B

C

1. C
2. ______
3. ______
4. ______
5. ______
6. ______

Grammar Connection: Simple Present Tense - *have*

<table>
<tr><td>I
You
We
They</td><td>have</td><td rowspan="2">brown hair.
long hair.
curly hair.</td></tr>
<tr><td>He
She</td><td>has</td></tr>
</table>

D **Complete the sentences with *have* or *has*. Then, write the letter of the correct picture(s) next to each sentence.**

A

B

C

D

E

F

1. She ______________ shoulder length hair. B
2. She ______________ a ponytail. ____
3. They ______________ black hair. ____ ____ ____
4. She ______________ braids. ____
5. They ______________ short hair. ____ ____
6. She ______________ glasses. ____
7. They ______________ long hair. ____ ____ ____

E **Complete with information about your hair.**

1. I have [black brown red blond gray] hair.
2. It's [long short shoulder-length].
3. My hair is [curly straight wavy].

Daily Activities

A Complete this information about your daily schedule. Write the time you do each activity.

1. I get up at ____:____.
2. I eat lunch at ____:____.
3. I do homework at ____:____.
4. I go to bed at ____:____.

B Circle the two words that can follow each verb.

1. take:	a walk	a lunch	a shower
2. eat:	lunch	coffee break	dinner
3. do:	homework	a shower	housework
4. go:	wake up	to bed	home
5. get:	makeup	dressed	up
6. take:	a nap	a break	a bed
7. have:	awake	breakfast	lunch

C Put your morning and evening activities in order. Cross out the things you do not do.

In the Morning

____ I brush my teeth.
____ I go to work/school.
____ I eat breakfast.
____ I get dressed.
____ I take a shower.
____ I comb my hair.
__1__ I get up.

In the Evening

____ I watch television.
____ I eat dinner.
____ I do homework.
____ I exercise.
____ I go to bed.
____ I make dinner.
____ I do housework.

Grammar Connection: Simple Present Tense with *I*

I	**work.** **take** a shower. **make** dinner.

I	**don't work.** **don't take** a shower. **don't make** dinner.

Note:

- The present tense tells about repeated or daily activities.

D Circle the correct verb. Make the sentence true for *you*.

1. I **get up** / **don't get up** at 6:00.
2. I **take** / **don't take** a shower in the morning.
3. I **eat** / **don't eat** breakfast.
4. I **go** / **don't go** to work.
5. I **exercise** / **don't exercise**.
6. I **do** / **don't do** homework every day.
7. I **make** / **don't make** dinner.
8. I **do** / **don't do** housework on the weekend.
9. I **watch** / **don't watch** television every night.
10. I **sleep** / **don't sleep** eight hours a night.

CD 1
Track 17

E Listen. Circle the correct answer.

1.	**a.** I wake up at 7:00.	**b.** I walk at 7:00.
2.	**a.** Yes, I take a shower in the morning.	**b.** Yes, I take a bath in the morning.
3.	**a.** Yes, I eat breakfast every day.	**b.** Yes, I eat lunch every day.
4.	**a.** I go to work at 9:00.	**b.** I go to bed at 9:00.
5.	**a.** Yes, I take a nap.	**b.** Yes, I take a break.
6.	**a.** I do my homework on Friday.	**b.** I do the housework on Friday.
7.	**a.** Yes, we eat dinner together.	**b.** Yes, we eat lunch together.
8.	**a.** Yes, I work every day.	**b.** Yes, I work out every day.
9.	**a.** I wash my hair after dinner.	**b.** I watch television after dinner.
10.	**a.** I go to bed at 11:00.	**b.** I go home at 11:00.

Walk, Jump, Run

A **Write the word for each action.**

run	fall	~~crawl~~	kneel

1. crawl
2. ______
3. ______
4. ______

Grammar Connection: Present Progressive Tense

I	**am**	
He She It	**is**	**walking.** **falling** **sitting down.**
We You They	**are**	

Note:

- The present progressive tense tells about an action that is happening now.

B **Read the sentences. Underline the complete present progressive verb.**

1. The woman <u>is entering</u> the building.
2. The boy is riding in a wagon.
3. The children are following their teacher.
4. The woman is going up the stairs.
5. The man is running for the bus.
6. The man is crossing the street.
7. The men are walking to the coffee shop.

C Match the opposites.

d	1. get in	a.	run
___	2. enter	b.	go up
___	3. walk	c.	leave
___	4. get on	d.	get out
___	5. sit down	e.	get off
___	6. go down	f.	pull
___	7. push	g.	stand up

CD 1
Track 18

D Look at the picture. Listen to each question and write the name of the correct person.

1. Tony is.
2. ________________
3. ________________
4. ________________
5. ________________
6. ________________
7. ________________
8. ________________
9. ________________

Feelings

A **How does each person feel? Write the correct word under each picture.**

angry	~~nervous~~	thirsty
tired	sick	happy

1. nervous

2. ______

3. ______

4. ______

5. ______

6. ______

B **Look at the pictures in your dictionary. Write the number of the correct person or people.**

1. The man is thirsty. He wants a soda. 8
2. The man is angry. ____
3. The man is thinking about his family in Mexico. He's homesick. ____
4. The man and woman are in love. ____
5. The man ran far, so he's tired. ____
6. The woman is uncomfortable on the rock. ____
7. The woman is worried because her daughter is sick. ____
8. The woman is thinking about lunch. She's hungry. ____
9. The boy is sad. He dropped his ice cream. ____
10. The man is afraid of the big dog. ____

Grammar Connection: Present Tense - *be*

I	**am**	tired. hungry. nervous.
He She It	**is**	
You We They	**are**	

C Complete the sentences with *am*, *is*, or *are* and an adjective from the dictionary. How does each person feel?

1. Eliza and Laura miss their families. They are homesick.
2. Li Ting's father is very sick. She ________.
3. Adam sees a big dog. He ________.
4. Manolo is not interested in the movie. He ________.
5. It's 4:00 Eva didn't eat lunch. She ________.
6. The students have a big test today. They ________.
7. Salim can't understand his homework. He ________.
8. Yana and Janet worked hard all day. They ________.

D Match the opposites.

b	**1.** happy	**a.** bored
____	**2.** comfortable	**b.** sad
____	**3.** interested	**c.** hungry
____	**4.** full	**d.** uncomfortable

CD 1
Track 19

E Listen. How does each person feel?

1. **a.** bored **b.** embarrassed
2. **a.** comfortable **b.** angry
3. **a.** proud **b.** calm
4. **a.** in love **b.** full
5. **a.** worried **b.** tired
6. **a.** surprised **b.** thirsty
7. **a.** calm **b.** sick
8. **a.** lonely **b.** nervous
9. **a.** comfortable **b.** frustrated
10. **a.** homesick **b.** scared

Wave, Greet, Smile

A Look at the pictures in your dictionary. Write the number of the correct picture.

1. She is giving a gift to her husband. __7__
2. She is having a conversation with her friend. ____
3. He is helping his son put on the helmet. ____
4. This husband and wife are arguing. ____
5. She is kissing her daughter. ____
6. She is inviting her friends for dinner. ____
7. She is writing a letter to a friend. ____
8. Two business people are shaking hands. ____
9. He is apologizing because he forgot her birthday. ____
10. She is complimenting her friend. ____
11. She is introducing her husband to her boss. ____
12. She is waving to a friend. ____

B Match the statement and the action.

__c__	1. "You will be OK."	a.	He is disagreeing with a friend.
____	2. "Hello! Come in!"	b.	She is inviting a friend to her party.
____	3. *Dear John,*	c.	She is comforting a friend.
____	4. "I don't think so."	d.	He is complimenting a friend.
____	5. "I think so, too."	e.	She is welcoming some friends.
____	6. "Can you come?"	f.	She is writing a letter to a friend.
____	7. "Hi, Mark. This is Tom."	g.	He is agreeing with a friend.
____	8. "You look wonderful!"	h.	He is calling a friend.

Grammar Connection: Present Progressive Tense

I	**am**	
He She It	**is**	wav**ing**. danc**ing**. smil**ing**.
We You They	**are**	

Note:
- The present progressive tense tells about an action that is happening now.

C Write the action next to the correct statement.

She is apologizing to a friend.	He is helping a friend.
They are arguing.	I'm greeting a friend.
I'm congratulating a friend.	She is introducing a friend.

1. "Wonderful! You got the job! I'm congratulating a friend.
2. "I'm sorry." ______
3. "Let me carry that for you." ______
4. "You never listen to me!" ______
5. I'd like you to meet my friend." ______
6. Hi, Paul. How are you?" ______

CD 1
Track 20

D Listen to each sentence. Write the number of the sentence under the correct picture.

a. ______

b. ______

c. ______

d. ______

e. 1

f. ______

Documents

A **Look at the documents in your dictionary. Write two documents under each category.**

Travel	School	Driving
visa	________	________
________	________	________

B **Look at the documents in your dictionary. Write the correct document or card for each event.**

1. When you are born: birth certificate
2. When you pass your driving test: ________
3. When you graduate from high school: ________
4. When you get married: ________
5. When you graduate from college: ________
6. When you start a job: ________
7. When you want to travel: ________
8. When you become a citizen: ________

C **Complete this form with your own information.**

Personal Information *(please print)*

Name ________
LAST FIRST MIDDLE INITIAL

Sex Male ☐ Female ☐

Date of birth ____ / ____ / ____
MONTH DAY YEAR

Place of birth ________

Soc. Sec. No. ________

Telephone No. ____ / ________
AREA CODE

E-mail ________

Grammar Connection: Possessive Adjectives

I - my	She - her
You - your	We - our
He - his	They - their

Note:

- Use a noun after a possessive adjective.

  My book is on the table. **His** car is black. **Her** name is Emma.

D **Look at the documents in your dictionary. Complete with *my*, *your*, *his*, *her*, or *their*.**

1. John Hong was born is California. __His__ date of birth is 6/21/1970.
2. ________ e-mail is jhong@bower.com.
3. ________ wife's name is Susan.
4. Susan was not born in the United States. ________ native country is Korea.
5. ________ date of birth is 01/05/1974.
6. John and Susan live in San Jose. ________ address is 452 Austin Street.
7. They have a daughter. ________ name is Karen.
8. What is your name? __My__________________________.
9. What is your e-mail address? ____________________________.
10. What is your date of birth? ____________________________.

CD 1 Track 21

E **Read the list of documents. Listen and write the number of each request next to the correct document.**

a. passport ____
b. student ID ____
c. driver's license __1__
d. marriage certificate ____
e. vehicle registration card ____
f. business card ____
g. green card ____
h. high school diploma ____

Nationalities

A **Look in your dictionary. Write the nationality.**

1. Nigeria	Nigerian	**8.** Spain	______
2. Mexico	______	**9.** Italy	______
3. France	______	**10.** Colombia	______
4. Australia	______	**11.** Korea	______
5. Venezuela	______	**12.** Turkey	______
6. United Kingdom	______	**13.** Peru	______
7. Germany	______	**14.** United States	______

B **Look in your dictionary. Complete the information about each flag. Write the nationality and colors.**

1.  The ___Brazilian___ flag is ___green,___ ___yellow, and blue___.

2.  The ______ flag is ______ ______.

3.  The ______ flag is ______ ______.

4.  The ______ flag is ______ ______.

5.  The ______ flag is ______ ______.

6. I am from ______.

The ______ flag is ______ ______.

Grammar Connection: Contractions with *be*

I'm	Peruvian. Chinese. Nigerian.
He's **She's** **It's**	
You're **We're** **They're**	

I am = I'm
He is = He's She is = She's It is = It's
You are = You're We are = We're They are = They're

C **Guess the nationality of each of these people. Use a contraction in your answer. (Check your answers at the bottom of the page.)**

Canadian	Japanese	Chinese	British
Iranian	Vietnamese	Indian	

1. Raj was born in New Delhi. He 's Indian.
2. Jack and Amy were born in Ottawa. They ________
3. Lan was born in Hanoi. She ________
4. Chen was born in Bejing. He ________
5. Charles was born in London. He ________
6. Mika was born is Tokyo. She ________
7. Ali and Asad were born in Tehran. They ________
8. I was born in ________. I ________

D **Listen and complete the sentences.**

CD 1
Track 21

Russian
Colombian
Greek
~~Thai~~
Japanese
Egyptian
Malaysian

1. Some ___Thai___ food is spicy.
2. Many ________ desserts are very sweet.
3. The Hermitage is a famous ________ museum.
4. ________ beaches are popular with tourists.
5. Shogatsu is the ________ New Year.
6. ________ coffee is delicious.
7. ________ history is very interesting.

Word Study

Study with a partner. Cover the word list. Your partner will say a word. Point to the correct picture.

Answers to Activity C: 1-Indian; 2-Canadian; 3-Vietnamese; 4-Chinese; 5-British; 6-Japanese; 7-Iranian; 8-Answers will vary.

Places Around Town

A Where does each person work?

church	police station	hospital
stadium	gas station	~~fire station~~

1. He works at a fire station.

2. He works at a ______________.

3. She works at a ______________.

4. He works at a ______________.

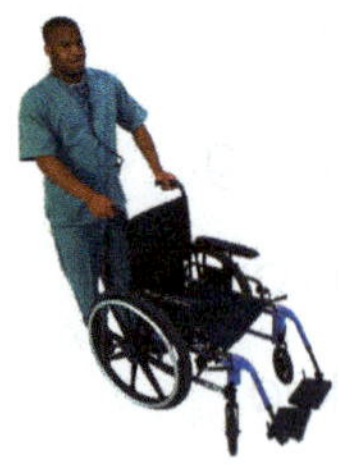

5. He works at a ______________.

6. He works at a ______________.

B Look at the places in your dictionary. Complete the sentences.

1. You can borrow a book from the library.
2. You can watch a movie at the ______________.
3. You can see a soccer game at the ______________.
4. You can stay overnight at the ______________.
5. You can get gas at the ______________.
6. You can mail a package at the ______________.
7. You can get a marriage license at ______________.
8. You can park your car in the ______________.
9. You can buy a car at the ______________.

Grammar Connection: Prepositions of Place

The fire station is **next to** city hall.
City hall is **between** the fire station and the library.
The fire truck is **in front of** the fire station.
The park is **across from** the library.

C Look at the town in your dictionary. Complete the sentences with *next to*, *between*, *in front of*, or *across from*.

1. The library is ___next to___ the courthouse.
2. The car dealership is ____________ the first station.
3. The school bus is ____________ the school.
4. The parking garage is ____________ the high-rise.
5. The flag is ____________ the post office.
6. The post office is ____________ the office building.
7. The library is ____________ the city hall and the courthouse.
8. The mosque is ____________ the motel.
9. The synagogue is ____________ the school.
10. Five police cars are ____________ the police station.

D Write each place in the correct group.

~~a church~~	~~a theater~~	a stadium	a synagogue
~~a fire station~~	a college	a movie theater	a mosque
~~a school~~	a police station	a hospital	

Education	Emergencies	Religion	Entertainment
a school	a fire station	a church	a theater
____________	____________	____________	____________
	____________	____________	____________

CD 1
Track 23

E Listen. Where is each person? Write the place.

1. ___library___
2. ____________
3. ____________
4. ____________
5. ____________
6. ____________
7. ____________
8. ____________
9. ____________
10. ____________

Shops and Stores

A **Look in your dictionary. Where can you buy the following items? Write the name of the correct store under each item.**

1. jewelry store

2. ____________

3. ____________

4. ____________

5. ____________

6. ____________

7. ____________

8. ____________

9. ____________

B **Circle two places you can buy each item or service.**

1. A ball:	a bookstore	a toy store	a sporting goods store
2. A dress:	a clothing store	a jewelry store	a department store
3. A haircut:	a barbershop	a laundromat	a hair salon
4. Bread:	a bakery	a supermarket	a clothing store
5. A cup of coffee:	a copy shop	a coffee shop	a fast food restaurant

Grammar Connection: Present Progressive Tense

I	**am**		
You	**are**		the electronics store.
He	**is**	**going to**	the dry cleaner.
She	**is**		the flea market.
We	**are**		
They	**are**		

Note:

- The present progressive tense talks about an action that is happening now.

C Where is each person going?

1. Tammy needs to get a dictionary. *She's going to the bookstore.*
2. Gina and Carl have to wash clothes. ____________________
3. I need to buy food for dinner. ____________________
4. Emma wants a manicure. ____________________
5. Jack needs a haircut. ____________________
6. I need a laptop computer. ____________________
7. Lana and Tess want a dog. ____________________
8. I need sneakers. ____________________

CD 1
Track 24

D Listen to each shopper. Complete each sentence with the correct shop or store.

1. She's at the *copy shop*.
2. He's at the ____________________.
3. He's at the ____________________.
4. She's at the ____________________.
5. He's at the ____________________.
6. She's at the ____________________.
7. He's at the ____________________.
8. He's at the ____________________.
9. She's at the ____________________.

ice cream stand
health club
~~copy shop~~
music store
bakery
drugstore
flower stand
beauty salon
dry cleaner

Bank

A Complete the sentences.

cash	~~ATM~~	vault
deposit	safe-deposit box	bankcard
security guard	teller window	passbook

1. The man is at an ATM.
2. He is putting his ______________ in the ATM.
3. He wants ______________.

4. The woman is at a ______________.
5. She is holding her ______________.
6. She is making a ______________.

7. The man is in the ______________.
8. He is opening his ______________.
9. The ______________ is standing in front of the vault.

B Circle the correct word.

1. I receive a [statement   vault] every month.
2. I need to [make   withdraw] a deposit.
3. Insert your [bankcard   checkbook] in the ATM.
4. I need a [customer   money order] for $50.
5. The [balance   bankcard] in our account is $1,000.
6. I pay my telephone bill by [interest   check].
7. I use the [drive-up window   deposit] at my bank.

Grammar Connection: *I'd like to*

I would like to I'd like to	order new checks.

Note:

- *Would like* means want.
- *I'd like* is the contraction for *I would like*. In conversation, use *I'd like*.

C What do you want to do at the bank? Write sentences using the cues and *I'd like to*.

1. apply for a loan — I'd like to apply for a loan.
2. open an account ______
3. deposit a check ______
4. withdraw some money ______
5. rent a safe-deposit box ______
6. get a money order ______

D Listen and circle the correct answer.

CD 1
Track 25

1. a. Yes, I have a savings account. (b.) Yes, I have a checking account.
2. a. in my safe-deposit box b. in my checking account
3. a. in the vault b. in the line
4. a. 5% b. $500
5. a. 1234-5678-0000 b. $1,800
6. a. 1234-5678-0000 b. $1,800
7. a. I pay my balance. b. I pay by money order.
8. a. Yes, I have a bankcard. b. Yes, I have a savings account.

E Answer these questions about your banking.

1. Do you have a checking account? Yes No
2. Do you have a savings account? Yes No
3. Do you receive a monthly statement in the mail? Yes No
4. Does your bank have a drive-up window? Yes No
5. Do you have an ATM card? Yes No
6. Do you have a safe-deposit box? Yes No

Post Office

A Circle the items you can send or receive in the mail.

bill	mailbox	package	postcard
greeting card	scale	catalog	mail truck
clerk	letter	overnight mail	zip code

B Write the word for each part of this letter.

envelope	zip code	return address
address	stamp	

5. ______________

1. ______________

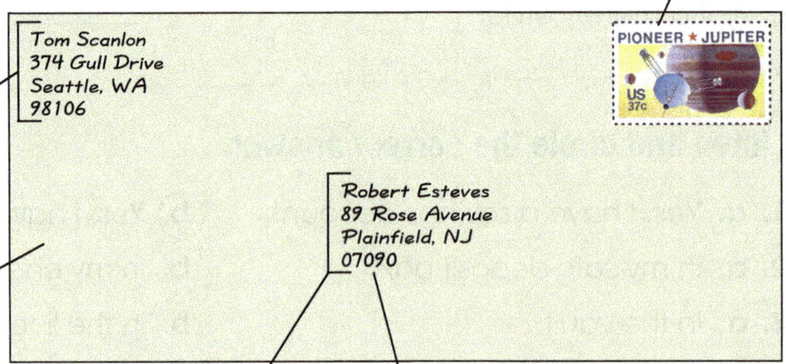

2. ______________

3. ______________

4. ______________

C Circle the correct word.

1. Put the letters in the [mailbox   mail carrier].
2. I need a(n) [postcard   envelope] for this letter.
3. I don't have a [stamp   clerk] for this envelope.
4. We received the telephone [zip code   bill] in the mail.
5. It's my mother's birthday. I'm sending her a [postmark   greeting card].
6. The [clerk   catalog] helps customers in the post office.
7. When I'm on vacation, I send [postmarks   postcards] to my family.
8. The clerk weighs packages on a [stamp machine   scale].

Grammar Connection: *First, Then, Next, Finally*

To obtain a post office box:
First, go to the post office with two forms of ID.
Next, fill out the application form.
Then, decide the box size you need.
Next, pay for the box.
Finally, take the key or the combination.

Note:
- Use these words to describe the order you do things in.

D Write the directions in the correct order.

bring the package to the post office	pay the postage
the clerk will tell you the postage	fill out the mailing label
the clerk will weigh the package	~~prepare the package~~

1. First, prepare the package.
2. Next, ______
3. Then, ______
4. Next, ______
5. Then, ______
6. Finally, ______

E Listen to each statement. Write the word you hear.

CD 1
Track 26

1. letter
2. ______
3. ______
4. ______
5. ______
6. ______
7. ______

zip code
stamp
~~letter~~
mailing address
mailbox
envelope
return address

Library

A **Complete the sentences.**

atlas	newspaper	biography	~~autobiography~~
cookbook	dictionary	magazine	picture book

1. You can read the story of a person's life by that person in an autobiography.
2. You can find the definitions of words in a ______________.
3. You can find recipes in a ______________.
4. You can read the story of a person's life in a ______________.
5. You can read the daily news in a ______________.
6. You can read a story to a child from a ______________.
7. You can find maps of different countries in an ______________.
8. You can read new articles every week or month in a ______________.

B **In which section will you find each book or periodical? Write the section under each book.**

reference section	fiction section
periodical section	nonfiction section

1. fiction section

2. ______________

3. ______________

4. ______________

5. ______________

6. ______________

Grammar Connection: Plural Nouns

Singular Nouns	Plural Nouns
a book	books
a dictionary	dictionaries
an encyclopedia	encyclopedias

Note:

- Use *a* or *an* with singular nouns.
- Some nouns are irregular in English. For example:

  a man – men a woman – women

  a child – children a person – people

C Look at the library in the dictionary. Circle the correct noun.

1. There is an [atlas / atlases] on the circulation desk.
2. There are some [person / people] in the library.
3. There are [computer / computers] in the library.
4. There is a [child / children] in the children's section.
5. There are some [newspaper / newspapers] in the periodical section.
6. There is a [woman / women] at the circulation desk.
7. There are many [book / books] in the fiction section.
8. There is a large [dictionary / dictionaries] on the table.

CD 1
Track 27

D Listen to each statement. Write the word you hear.

1. author
2. ______
3. ______
4. ______
5. ______
6. ______
7. ______
8. ______

library card
~~author~~
headline
atlas
librarian
autobiography
title
reading room

E Complete this information.

1. There [is isn't] a library in my town.
2. I can check out books for ____ weeks.
3. I [have don't have] a library card.
4. My school [has doesn't have] a library.
5. I like to read [fiction nonfiction] books.

Daycare Center

A Write the words in the correct category.

a bib	~~powder~~	a diaper	a rest mat	a crib
formula	baby wipes	a playpen	a high chair	

1. Things you can use when you change a baby:	2. Things you can use when you feed a baby:	3. Places a baby can sleep:
powder	______	______
______	______	______
______	______	______

B Match.

c	**1.** baby	**a.** pail		*c*	**1.** cloth	**a.** table
____	**2.** disposable	**b.** chair		____	**2.** diaper	**b.** ring
____	**3.** potty	**c.** swing		____	**3.** changing	**c.** diaper
____	**4.** training	**d.** diaper		____	**4.** high	**d.** pin
____	**5.** diaper	**e.** pants		____	**5.** teething	**e.** chair

C Look at the daycare center in your dictionary. Circle *T* for true or *F* for false.

1. A girl and a boy are playing on the floor.	(T)	F
2. There is a child in a stroller.	T	F
3. This center has infants, toddlers, and preschoolers.	T	F
4. One child is drinking from a bottle.	T	F
5. There are cubbies for the children's bags.	T	F
6. The child in the baby swing has a rattle.	T	F
7. Two children are sitting in high chairs.	T	F

Grammar Connection: Future Tense – *going to*

I	**am**	**going to**	**play** with the baby.
You	**are**		
He	**is**		
She	**is**		
We	**are**		
They	**are**		

Note:

- The future tense tells about things you plan to do tomorrow, next week, or some time in the future.

D Underline the future verb. Then, complete the sentences.

stroller	diaper	~~bottle~~
daycare center	crib	changing table

1. The baby is crying. He is going to give the baby a bottle.
2. The baby is tired. I am going to put the baby in his ________.
3. The baby is wet. He is going to put the baby on the ________ and change his ________.
4. We are going to take the baby for a walk in his ________.
5. When the baby is six months old, they are going to look for a good ________.

CD 1 Track 28

E Listen as Mrs. Chin talks to her babysitter. Write the number of the item you hear under the correct picture.

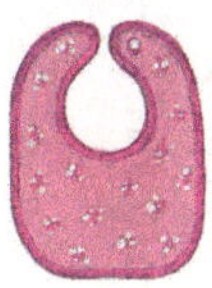

a. ________

b. ________

c. ________

d. ________

e. ________

f. ________

g. ________

h. 1

City Square

A **Write the word for each item.**

a streetlight	a statue	a sign
~~a fire hydrant~~	a parking meter	a monument

1. a fire hydrant
2. ____________
3. ____________

4. ____________
5. ____________
6. ____________

B **Look at the picture of the city square in your dictionary. Circle *T* if the statement is true. Circle *F* if the statement is false.**

1. Two pedestrians are crossing the street. (T) F
2. There is a statue in front of the museum. T F
3. There is a taxi in front of the hotel. T F
4. A man is leaving the travel agency. T F
5. The café is next to the museum. T F
6. A man is putting money in a parking meter. T F
7. The fountain is in front of the monument. T F
8. There is a car in the handicapped parking space. T F
9. A large billboard says "Keep Our City Clean!" T F
10. There is a street musician in front of the bank. T F

Grammar Connection: *Can*

I **can buy** a frame at the art gallery.
You **can cash** a check at the bank.

Note:

- Use *can* to show you are able to do something.
- Use the base form of the verb after *can*.

C Complete the sentences with *can* and the correct words.

plan a trip	stay overnight	get some cash	buy a newspaper
ask for directions	~~get a cup of coffee~~	look at paintings	buy a soda

1. You ___can get a cup of coffee___ at the café.
2. They ______________________ at a hotel.
3. You ______________________ at the information booth.
4. I ______________________ at the bank.
5. We ______________________ at the travel agency.
6. She ______________________ from the street vendor.
7. We ______________________ at the museum.
8. He ______________________ at the newsstand.

CD 1
Track 29

D Listen. Where is each person? Write the place.

1. ___museum___
2. ______________
3. ______________
4. ______________
5. ______________
6. ______________
7. ______________

café
travel agency
newsstand
tourist information booth
bank
hotel
~~museum~~

E Circle the places and things you can find in your city.

a statue	a monument	a tourist information booth
a hotel	a fountain	an art gallery
a travel agency	a newsstand	a museum

Crime and Justice

A **Write the word for the person or people.**

a jury	a judge	~~a police officer~~	a prisoner	a lawyer

1. a police officer

2. ______________

3. ______________

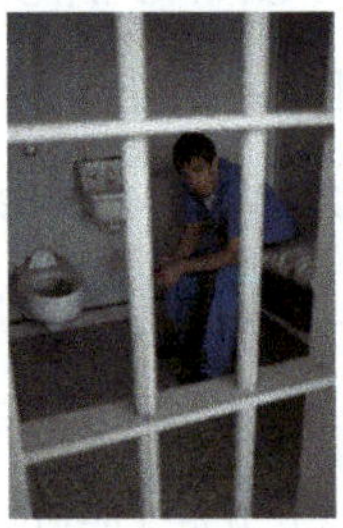

4. ______________

5. ______________

B **Circle the correct person.**

1. A [criminal   witness] commits a crime.
2. A [police officer   judge] arrests the criminal.
3. A [jury   witness] sees the crime.
4. A [judge   lawyer] defends the criminal.
5. A [jury   witness] decides if the person is guilty or not guilty.
6. A [prisoner   judge] can be in jail for many years.

Grammar Connection: Present Progressive Statements – Third Person Singular

He **is mugging** someone.
She **is bribing** a police officer.

C **Look at the crimes in your dictionary. Complete the description of the each crime in the present progressive. Then, write the name of the crime.**

1. He ___is starting___ (start) a fire. ___arson___
2. He ________________ (sell) drugs. ________________
3. He ________________ (take) a woman's purse. ________________
4. She ________________ (write) on a wall with spray paint. ________________
5. He ________________ (steal) a camera from a store. ________________
6. She ________________ (drink) and driving. ________________
7. He ________________ (steal) a car. ________________
8. He ________________ (take) jewelry from a house. ________________

CD 1
Track 30

D **Listen and complete the sentences with the word or words you hear.**

arson	auto theft	bribery	armed robbery
shoplifting	~~murder~~	drug dealing	drunk driving

1. The police arrested a woman for ___murder___.
2. A man is on trial for ________________.
3. The police stopped a woman for ________________.
4. The woman is in prison for ________________.
5. He is in jail for ________________.
6. The store stopped the woman for ________________.
7. The man is in jail for ________________.
8. The police arrested them for ________________.

Word Study

- Write each word you want to learn on one side of a note card.
- Write the word in your language on the other side.
- Put the cards in your pocket, bag, or backpack.
- Take out the cards a few times each day and study the new words.

Types of Homes

A Complete each sentence with the type of home you see.

houseboat	townhouse	tent
~~apartment~~	mobile home	log cabin

1. apartment

2. ______

3. ______

4. ______

5. ______

6. ______

B Match the description with the type of home.

c	**1.** a home on the water	**a.** a farmhouse
____	**2.** a home in a very cold area	**b.** a retirement home
____	**3.** a home on a farm	**c.** a houseboat
____	**4.** a home for two families	**d.** an apartment building
____	**5.** a home for older people	**e.** a duplex
____	**6.** a home for students	**f.** an igloo
____	**7.** a home that people can move	**g.** a dormitory
____	**8.** a building with many homes	**h.** a castle
____	**9.** a home for a king and queen	**i.** a mobile home

CD 1
Track 31

C **Read the list of words. Listen to each statement. Write the word you hear.**

house	condominium	retirement home	ranch
mobile home	duplex	~~apartment~~	farmhouse

1. My parents live in an ___apartment___ in the city.
2. My sister lives in a ______________ in the country.
3. My brother lives in a ______________ in a small town.
4. My cousin lives in a ______________ in the country.
5. I live in a ______________ in the suburbs.
6. My neighbors live in a ______________.
7. My friend lives in a ______________.
8. My grandparents live in a ______________ in a small town.

Grammar Connection: Simple Present Tense – *be*

Affirmative	Negative
A dorm room **is** small.	A dorm room **isn't** quiet.

D **Complete the sentences with *is* or *isn't*.**

1. An igloo ___isn't___ hot. It ______________ cold.
2. A castle ______________ easy to clean.
3. A palace ______________ large. It ______________ small.
4. An apartment in the city ______________ quiet.
5. A villa ______________ expensive.
6. A tent ______________ comfortable.
7. A city ______________ busy.
8. The country ______________ beautiful.

E **Complete with information about your city or town.**

1. I live in ______________________ (name of city or town).
2. I live in [a city   the suburbs   a small town   the country].
3. I live in a(n) ______________ (type of home).
4. There are many types of homes in my area. There are ______________, ______________, and ______________.

Finding a Place to Live

A **Look at page 64 in your dictionary. Write the number of the correct picture.**

1. She is unpacking her dishes. 11
2. She is making an appointment with the landlord. ____
3. Her friends are helping her load the van with boxes. ____
4. Her friends are helping her decorate the apartment. ____
5. She is looking for an apartment online. ____
6. She is meeting the neighbors. ____
7. She is getting the key from the landlord. ____
8. She is packing the boxes. ____

B **Circle the two words that can follow each verb.**

1. meet:	(a.) the landlord	b. the furniture	(c.) the neighbors
2. decorate:	a. the decision	b. the house	c. the apartment
3. pay:	a. the key	b. the rent	c. the security deposit
4. sign:	a. the lease	b. the price	c. the loan documents
5. make:	a. an offer	b. a down payment	c. the van
6. make:	a. a decision	b. an appointment	c. a price

C **Put the steps in order.**

Renting an Apartment

____ Sign the lease.
____ See an apartment you like.
____ Pay a security deposit.
____ Get the key.
1 Look for an apartment.

Buying a House

____ Make an offer.
____ Apply for a loan.
____ Make a decision.
1 Look at houses.
____ Negotiate the price.

Grammar Connection: Present Progressive Tense Statements

I	**am**	**calling** a real estate agent.
We	**are**	**looking** at houses.
They	**are**	**applying** for a loan.
He	**is**	**packing**.
She	**is**	**moving**.

Note:

- We use the present progressive tense to talk about actions that are happening now.

D **Complete the sentences. Use the present progressive form of the correct verb.**

arrange	ask	load	~~look~~
make	meet	pack	pay

1. I ___am looking___ for an apartment to rent.
2. He ____________ an appointment to see the apartment.
3. She ____________ questions about the apartment.
4. I ____________ the glasses in the boxes.
5. They ____________ the furniture into the truck.
6. We ____________ the furniture in the living room.
7. They ____________ the neighbors.
8. He ____________ the rent.

CD 1
Track 32

E **Listen to each conversation. Write the number of the conversation under the correct picture.**

a. ________

b. ________

c. ________

d. ________

e. ___1___

f. ________

g. ________

h. ________

Apartment Building

A **Complete the sentences.**

tenant	~~furnished apartment~~	studio
superintendent	roommate	unfurnished apartment

1. An apartment with furniture is a furnished apartment.
2. An apartment with no furniture is an ______________ apartment.
3. A ______________ is a small apartment with one room.
4. A ______________ rents an apartment.
5. A ______________ shares an apartment with another person.
6. A ______________ takes care of an apartment building.

B **Look at the apartment building in your dictionary. Circle *T* if the statement is true. Circle *F* if the statement is false.**

1. The workout room is in the basement. T (F)
2. The fire escape goes down into the courtyard. T F
3. The laundry room is in the basement. T F
4. All the apartments have air conditioners. T F
5. There is a doorman in front of the revolving door. T F
6. All of the apartments are furnished. T F
7. Every apartment has a balcony. T F
8. There is an elevator in the building. T F

CD 1
Track 33

C **Listen to this conversation between a landlord and a person looking for an apartment. Put a check (✓) next to the features the apartment has. Put an *X* next to the features the apartment doesn't have.**

X 1. air conditioner
____ 2. balcony
____ 3. fire escape
____ 4. dead-bolt lock
____ 5. peephole
____ 6. laundry room
____ 7. parking space
____ 8. elevator

Grammar Connection: Simple Present Tense - *has / doesn't have*

Affirmative	Negative
The building **has** an elevator.	The building **doesn't have** a doorman.

Note:

- The contraction for *does not* is *doesn't.*
- For the negative of *he, she,* and *it,* use *does not* and the base form of the verb.

D Complete the sentences with *has* or *doesn't have.*

1. This apartment ___doesn't have___ three bedrooms.
2. This building ________________ an elevator.
3. This apartment ________________ an air conditioner.
4. This building ________________ a laundry room.
5. This apartment ________________ two bedrooms.
6. This building ________________ an elevator.
7. This building ________________ a doorman.
8. This building ________________ parking.

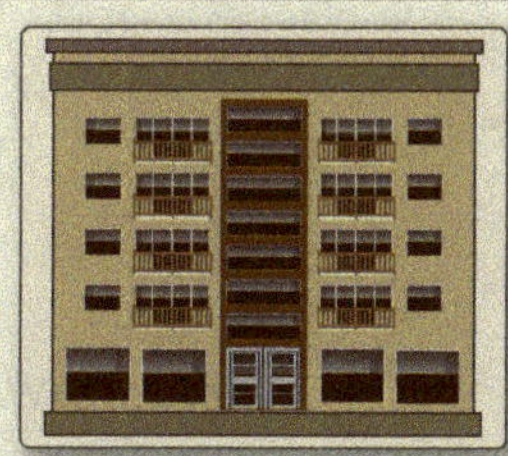

Two-bedroom apartment for rent.
Third floor
No elevator
Air conditioner
Laundry room

One-bedroom apartment for rent.
Elevator
Doorman
No parking

E You are looking for an apartment to rent. Rate these features from 1 (most important) to 8 (least important).

____ workout room

____ laundry room

____ storage locker

____ doorman

____ balcony

____ air conditioner

____ parking space

____ intercom

House and Garden

A Write the word for each house and garden item.

a hammock	a rake	a hose	a grill
a garbage can	hedge clippers	~~a lawn mower~~	a wheelbarrow

1. a lawn mower
2. __________
3. __________
4. __________

5. __________
6. __________
7. __________
8. __________

B Match.

e	1. lawn	a. bell
___	2. door	b. light
___	3. wheel	c. way
___	4. drive	d. barrow
___	5. sky	e. mower

C Look at the picture of the house and garden in your dictionary. Circle *T* if the statement is true. Circle *F* if the statement is false.

1. A man is mowing the lawn.	(T)	F
2. The rake is in the garage.	T	F
3. The front door is open.	T	F
4. A woman is working in the garden.	T	F
5. The sprinkler is on.	T	F
6. The deck is over the garage.	T	F

Grammar Connection: *Or* Questions

Is the yard large **or** small?	It's **large**. It's **small**.

D Put the words in the correct order to write a question. Then, write the answer.

the garden / large / or / is / small

1. Is the garden large or small? It's small.

or / full / is / empty / the wheelbarrow

2. ______________________? ______________

the garage door / is / open / closed / or

3. ______________________? ______________

is / clean / the garage / dirty / or

4. ______________________? ______________

CD 1
Track 34

E Look at the pictures of the two houses. Listen to each statement. Does it describe House A or House B?

A

B

1.	House A	House B	7.	House A	House B
2.	House A	House B	8.	House A	House B
3.	House A	House B	9.	House A	House B
4.	House A	House B	10.	House A	House B
5.	House A	House B	11.	House A	House B
6.	House A	House B	12.	House A	House B

Kitchen and Dining Area

A **Write the words for these kitchen items.**

a microwave	a coffeemaker	a drying rack	a bowl
a tea kettle	a stool	a blender	a mug
a glass	a spice rack	a toaster	~~a teapot~~

1. a teapot

2. ______________

3. ______________

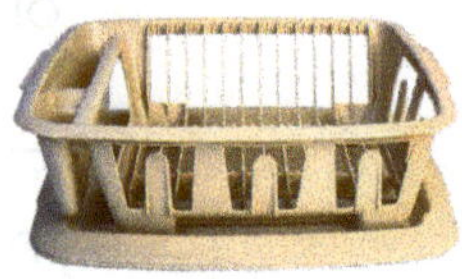
4. ______________

5. ______________

6. ______________

7. ______________

8. ______________

9. ______________

10. ______________

11. ______________

12. ______________

B **Look at the picture of the kitchen and dining area in your dictionary. Circle *T* if the statement is true. Circle *F* if the statement is false.**

1. The freezer door is open.	(T)	F
2. There are seven plates in the drying rack.	T	F
3. The microwave is above the stove.	T	F
4. The garbage disposal is under the sink.	T	F
5. The coffeemaker is next to the blender.	T	F
6. The oven door is open.	T	F
7. The stool is in front of the sink.	T	F
8. There is a candle on the table.	T	F

Grammar Connection: *There is / There are* Statements

There is	a cup on the table.
There are	two cups on the table.

C Look at the picture in your dictionary. Complete the sentences with *There is* or *There are*.

1. _____There is_____ is teapot on the table.
2. ______________ four dishes in the dish rack.
3. ______________ two glasses on the table.
4. ______________ a dish towel on the refrigerator.
5. ______________ two chairs at the table.
6. ______________ two bowls on the table.
7. ______________ a toaster on the counter.
8. ______________ sixteen spice jars in the spice rack.

CD 1
Track 35

D Look at the two place settings. Listen to each statement. Does it describe place setting A, place setting B, or both?

A

B

1.	(A)	(B)	6.	A	B
2.	A	B	7.	A	B
3.	A	B	8.	A	B
4.	A	B	9.	A	B
5.	A	B	10.	A	B

Living Room

A **Match.**

c	**1.** end	**a.** seat	____	**1.** window	**a.** switch
____	**2.** love	**b.** chair	____	**2.** smoke	**b.** table
____	**3.** ceiling	**c.** table	____	**3.** fire	**c.** seat
____	**4.** throw	**d.** fan	____	**4.** coffee	**d.** screen
____	**5.** rocking	**e.** pillow	____	**5.** light	**e.** detector

B **Follow the directions and complete the drawing.**

1. There is a ceiling fan over the sofa.

2. There is an end table to the right of the sofa.

3. There is a lamp on the end table.

4. There is a coffee table in front of the sofa.

5. There are two throw pillows on the sofa.

6. There is a big window behind the sofa.

7. There are curtains on the window. They are open.

8. There is a bookcase to the left of the sofa.

Grammar Connection: Preposition Review

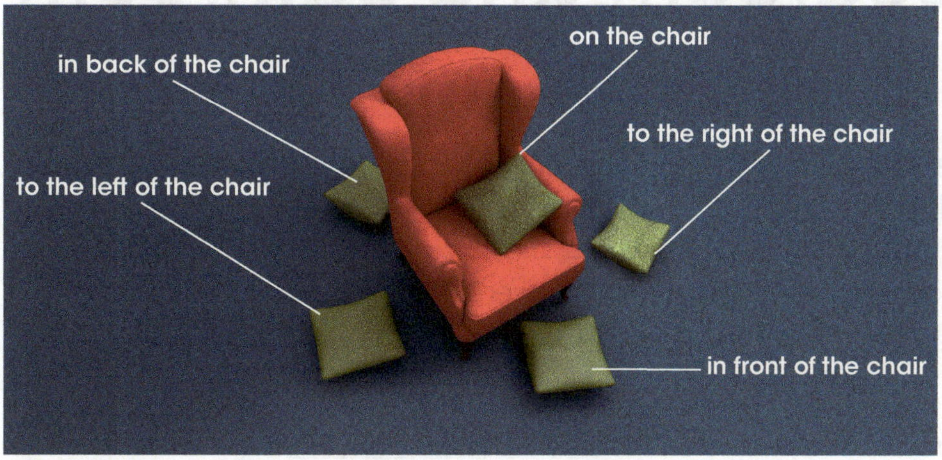

C **Look at the picture in your dictionary. Complete the sentences with the correct preposition.**

1. There is a coffee table ___in front of___ the sofa.
2. There are two pillows ______________ the window seat.
3. There is a cushion ______________ the bench.
4. There is an end table ______________ the sofa.
5. There are two magazines ______________ the coffee table.
6. There is a clock ______________ the mantel.
7. There is a rocking chair ______________ the fireplace.
8. There is an ottoman ______________ the loveseat.
9. There is a wall unit ______________ the sofa.
10. There is a bookcase ______________ the fireplace.

CD 1
Track 36

D **Listen to the conversations. Write the number of each conversation under the correct picture.**

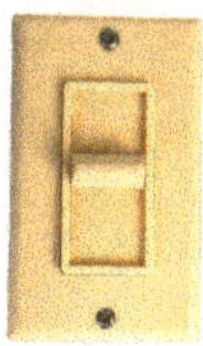

a. __________

b. __________

c. __________

d. __________

e. __________

f. _____1_____

g. __________

h. __________

Bedroom and Bathroom

A **Look at the pictures of the bedroom and bathroom in your dictionary. Complete the sentences.**

alarm clock	drawer	shower curtain	medicine cabinet
~~bed~~	rug	toilet paper	bedspread

1. There are two pillows on the ___bed___.
2. There is an ________ on the night table.
3. The ________ is purple.
4. The ________ is on the wall between the toilet and the bathtub.
5. The shower has a green ________.
6. There's a gray ________ on the floor in the bedroom.
7. One dresser ________ is open.
8. There's a ________ above the toilet.

B **Look at the pictures of the bedroom and bathroom in your dictionary. Match each item and its location.**

_e_	1. The wastebasket is	a. over the dresser.
____	2. The lamp is	b. on the bed.
____	3. The pillows are	c. between the tub and the toilet.
____	4. The plunger is	d. next to the bed.
____	5. The mirror is	e. under the sink.
____	6. The night table is	f. on the dresser.

C **Circle the items people often put on a bed.**

bedspread	mirror	rug	washcloth
dresser	pillow	faucet	comforter
blanket	sheet	drawer	pillowcase

Grammar Connection: *There is / There are* Questions and Answers

Questions	Answers	
Is there a lamp on the dresser?	Yes, **there is.**	No, **there isn't.**
Are there some clothes on the bed?	Yes, **there are.**	No, **there aren't.**

D **Look at the pictures of the bedroom and bathroom in your dictionary. Answer the questions.**

1. Is there a mirror over the dresser? Yes, there is.
2. Is there a lamp on the dresser? ____________
3. Is there a wastebasket in the bedroom? ____________
4. Are there some pillows on the bed? ____________
5. Are there some clothes on the bed? ____________
6. Is there a clock on the night table? ____________
7. Are there some keys on the dresser? ____________
8. Is there a closet in the bathroom? ____________
9. Is there a washcloth on the sink? ____________
10. Is there a medicine cabinet over the sink? ____________

CD 1
Track 37

E **Listen to the parent's instructions. Write the number of each sentence under the correct picture.**

a. ____________

b. ____________

c. 1

d. ____________

e. ____________

f. ____________

g. ____________

h. ____________

Household Problems

A Check the problems you see in the kitchen and the bathroom.

☐ **1.** The window is broken.

☐ **2.** The wall is cracked.

☐ **3.** The faucet drips.

☐ **4.** There are mice in the kitchen.

☐ **5.** There are ants in the kitchen.

☐ **1.** The bathroom is flooded.

☐ **2.** The toilet is clogged.

☐ **3.** The lightbulb is burned out.

☐ **4.** The lock is jammed.

☐ **5.** The ceiling leaks.

B Look at the house in your dictionary. Write the name of the correct person.

electrician	roofer	plumber	handyman	~~locksmith~~	meter reader

1. The ____locksmith____ is fixing the lock.

2. The ________________ is checking the gas meter.

3. The ________________ is putting in a new light bulb.

4. The ________________ is fixing the roof.

5. The ________________ is checking the breaker panel.

6. The ________________ is fixing the toilet.

Grammar Connection: Modal - *should*

You **should call** a plumber.
You **should call** a locksmith.

Note:
- Use *should* to give advice or a suggestion.
- Use the base form of the verb after *should*.

C **Read the problems below. Match the problem with the correct person or company.**

1. The power is out. __d__
2. We have termites. ____
3. The lock is jammed. ____
4. The faucet drips. ____
5. The window is broken. ____
6. The toilet is clogged. ____
7. We have cockroaches. ____
8. The roof leaks. ____

a. You should call a plumber.
b. You should call an exterminator.
c. You should call a handyman.
d. You should call an electrician.
e. You should call a roofer.
f. You should call a locksmith.

CD 1
Track 38

D **Listen to each problem. Who is each person talking to?**

1. **a.** an exterminator **b.** a roofer **(c.)** a plumber
2. **a.** a meter reader **b.** an exterminator **c.** an electrician
3. **a.** a locksmith **b.** a plumber **c.** a roofer
4. **a.** an electrician **b.** a roofer **c.** a meter reader
5. **a.** a plumber **b.** an exterminator **c.** an electrician
6. **a.** a handyman **b.** a roofer **c.** a plumber
7. **a.** an exterminator **b.** a plumber **c.** a meter reader

Household Chores

A **Name two chores that people do in each of these rooms or areas.**

Living room: vacuum the carpet ____________ ____________

Bedroom: ____________ ____________

Bathroom: ____________ ____________

Kitchen: ____________ ____________

Outside: ____________ ____________

B **Circle the correct word.**

1. [Clean Empty] the wastebasket.
2. [Put away Dust] the dishes.
3. [Wipe Do] the laundry.
4. [Mop Polish] the furniture.
5. [Pay Throw away] the bills.
6. [Dry Change] the dishes.
7. [Wipe Shake out] the rug.
8. [Clean Take out] the sink.
9. [Mow Rake] the leaves.
10. [Do Weed] the garden.

C **Read each sentence pair. If the meaning is the *same*, write *S*. If the meaning is *different*, write *D*.**

1. Do the laundry.	Wash the clothes.	S
2. Change the sheets.	Dry the sheets.	______
3. Mow the lawn.	Mow the grass.	______
4. Weed the garden.	Water the garden.	______
5. Wash the dishes.	Put away the dishes.	______
6. Take out the trash.	Put the trash outside.	______
7. Vacuum the carpet.	Wash the carpet.	______
8. Do the dishes.	Wash the dishes.	______

Grammar Connection: Polite Requests

Please do the dishes.
Please fold the clothes.

Note:
- Most polite requests start with *Please*.
- Use the base form of the verb to make requests.

D Write the correct request under each picture. Begin each request with *Please*.

sweep the floor	scrub the toilet	take out the trash
~~rake the leaves~~	do the laundry	put away the dishes

1. Please rake the leaves.

2. ______________________

3. ______________________

4. ______________________

5. ______________________

6. ______________________

CD 1
Track 39

E Listen to a mother talk with her children. Draw a line from each child to the chores the mother gives him.

1. Jason
2. Kevin
3. Mike

a. Do the dishes.
b. Mow the grass.
c. Vacuum the carpets.
d. Polish the furniture.
e. Mop the floor.
f. Empty the wastebaskets.

Cleaning Supplies

A Look in your dictionary. Write two supplies that you need for each job.

1. a vacuum
   a vacuum cleaner bag

2. ______________
   ____

3. ______________
   ____

4. ______________
   ____

5. ______________
   ____

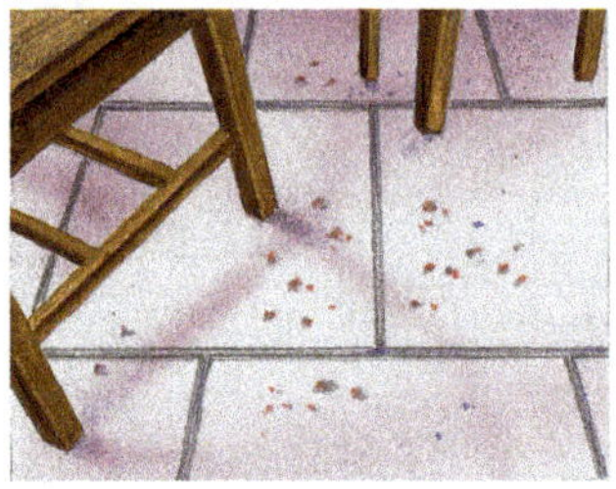

6. ______________
   ____

B Complete the sentences.

bucket	trash bag	recycling bin
dishwasher detergent	~~rubber gloves~~	vacuum cleaner bag

1. Put rubber gloves on your hands when you wash the dishes.
2. Put some water in the ______________.
3. Put a new ______________ in the vacuum cleaner.
4. Put some ______________ in the dishwasher.
5. Don't put the empty bottles in the trash bag. Put them in the ______________.
6. Put a new ______________ in the basket.

CD 1
Track 40

C Listen to each conversation. Write the item that each family needs.

1. dishwasher detergent
2. ______________
3. ______________
4. ______________
5. ______________
6. ______________
7. ______________
8. ______________
9. ______________

glass cleaner
flyswatter
mousetraps
~~dishwasher detergent~~
dish soap
garbage bags
scouring pads
vacuum cleaner bags
furniture polish

Grammar Connection: *This / These*

Put **this** rag in the pail.
Put **these** rags in the pail.

Note:

- Use *this* for singular nouns.
- Use *these* for plural nouns.

D Circle the correct word, *this* or *these*.

1. Put [this / these] mop in the closet.
2. Put [this / these] rubber gloves next to the sink.
3. Put [this / these] sponges under the sink.
4. Put [this / these] bug spray on the top shelf.
5. Put [this / these] paper towels in the kitchen.
6. Put [this / these] trash bag in the basket.
7. Put [this / these] dustpan in the cabinet.
8. Put [this / these] vacuum cleaner bags in the closet.
9. Put [this / these] sponge in the sink.
10. Put [this / these] scrub brush next to the pail.

Word Study

Make a word wall. When you learn a new word, stick it on the wall (or refrigerator, or mirror, or any other place where you often look). Look at the new words several times a day. When you know a word, take it down. Continue to add new words you need to study.

Fruits and Nuts

A Complete the crossword puzzle.

Across

1 

2 

4 

6 

7 

8 

9 

10 

11 

Down

1 

3 

5 

8 

B Cross out the word that does not belong.

1. lemons	limes	~~pears~~
2. pecans	almonds	bananas
3. olives	grapefruit	oranges
4. strawberries	blueberries	cherries
5. peaches	pears	peanuts

Grammar Connection: *This / These*

Singular	Plural
This banana is ripe.	**These** bananas are ripe.
This plum is juicy.	**These** plums are juicy.

Note:

- Use *this* with singular nouns.
- Use *these* with plural nouns.

C Change the singular sentences to plural.

1. This pear is ripe. These pears are ripe.
2. This strawberry is juicy. ______
3. This mango is delicious. ______
4. This watermelon is big. ______
5. This melon is ripe. ______
6. This kiwi is delicious. ______
7. This orange is juicy. ______

CD 1 Track 41

D Listen to each conversation. Which fruit is each speaker talking about?

1.	**a.** pear	**b.** apple	**c.** apricot
2.	**a.** plum	**b.** peach	**c.** pear
3.	**a.** grapes	**b.** figs	**c.** dates
4.	**a.** lime	**b.** lemon	**c.** almonds
5.	**a.** peanuts	**b.** walnuts	**c.** watermelon
6.	**a.** avocado	**b.** papaya	**c.** pomegranate
7.	**a.** raspberry	**b.** blueberry	**c.** strawberry
8.	**a.** avocado	**b.** apricot	**c.** orange
9.	**a.** cherries	**b.** pecans	**c.** kiwis
10.	**a.** almonds	**b.** olives	**c.** apples

E Complete each sentence with the name of a fruit or nut.

1. I like ______. I don't like ______.
2. ______ are my favorite fruit.
3. ______ are my favorite nuts.
4. I like ______ pie.

Vegetables

A Find the words.

C	U	C	U	M	B	E	R	E	N
O	T	E	G	G	P	L	A	N	T
L	O	L	P	E	A	S	D	R	O
E	B	E	G	A	R	L	I	C	M
T	U	R	N	I	P	A	S	B	A
T	O	Y	C	O	R	N	H	E	T
U	F	P	O	T	A	T	O	E	O
C	A	B	B	A	G	E	R	T	W
E	S	P	I	N	A	C	H	S	I

~~cucumber~~	garlic
spinach	celery
turnip	lettuce
eggplant	tomato
cabbage	potato
radish	peas
corn	beets

Grammar Connection: *How much* with *be*

How much	**is**	the spinach?	**It's**	$1.99 a pound.
How much	**are**	the onions?	**They're**	79¢ a pound.

Note:
- The contraction for *It is*: *It's*.
- The contraction for *They are*: *They're*.

B Complete the answers with *It's* or *They're*.

1. How much is the cauliflower? ____________ $1.59 a pound.
2. How much are the potatoes? ____________ 69¢ a pound.
3. How much are the kidney beans? ____________ $1.19 a pound.
4. How much is the squash? ____________ 79¢ a pound.
5. How much is the garlic? ____________ 99¢ a pound.
6. How much are the tomatoes? ____________ $1.29 a pound.
7. How much are the peas? ____________ $1.49 a pound.

C **Look at the supermarket ad. Write the word for each vegetable on the line below the vegetable.**

asparagus	mushrooms	spinach
cabbage	peas	potatoes
artichokes	scallions	~~celery~~

D **Look at the ad above and listen for the price of each item. Write the price of the item in the box below the vegetable.**

CD 1
Track 42

Meat, Poultry, and Seafood

A **Write the word for each fish or shellfish.**

crab	lobster	scallops	oysters
trout	salmon	shrimp	~~clams~~

1. clams

2. ______

3. ______

4. ______

5. ______

6. ______

7. ______

8. ______

B **Unscramble each word. What is the fish or shellfish?**

1. stsyore oysters
2. shprim ______
3. ttour ______
4. doc ______
5. loberts ______
6. brac ______
7. slaomn ______
8. scalm ______
9. aunt ______
10. messuls ______

C **Write the names of your two favorite kinds of meat, poultry, and seafood.**

Meat: ______ ______

Poultry: ______ ______

Seafood: ______ ______

Grammar Connection: Simple Present Tense – Affirmative and Negative

Affirmative		
I	like	chicken.
He	eats	pork.
She	buys	oysters.
They	like	salami.

Negative		
I	don't like	chicken.
He	doesn't eat	pork.
She	doesn't buy	oysters.
They	don't like	salami.

D Write the negative form of each sentence.

1. I like pork chops. _I don't like pork chops._
2. They eat meat. ______________
3. He likes shrimp. ______________
4. She buys clams. ______________
5. They like sausages. ______________
6. I eat steak. ______________
7. He eats liver. ______________

CD 1
Track 43

E Listen and complete.

1. two pounds of _ground beef_
2. a small piece of ______________
3. four ______________
4. a large ______________
5. six ______________
6. three ______________
7. one pound of ______________
8. two ______________
9. a six- or seven-pound ______________
10. a small ______________

chicken
chicken breasts
veal cutlets
shrimp
tuna
~~ground beef~~
roast beef
pork roast
chicken legs
pork chops

F Write the names of two of your favorite dishes. What kind of meat, poultry, or seafood is in each?

______________ has ______________ in it.

______________ has ______________ in it.

Inside the Refrigerator

A **Write the word for each food item.**

orange juice	salad	jam	bacon
a waffle	~~cheese~~	cold cuts	pickles

1. *cheese*

2. ____________

3. ____________

4. ____________

5. ____________

6. ____________

7. ____________

8. ____________

B **Look at the refrigerator in your dictionary. Where is each food item in the refrigerator?**

on the top shelf	in the freezer
on the middle shelf	in the door
on the bottom shelf	

1. The yogurt is *on the middle shelf*.
2. The milk is ____________.
3. The ice cream is ____________.
4. The eggs are ____________.
5. The salad is ____________.
6. The tofu is ____________.
7. The frozen vegetables are ____________.
8. The syrup is ____________.
9. The cream is ____________.

Grammar Connection: Count and Non-count Nouns

Count Nouns	
Singular	**Plural**
an egg	some eggs
an orange	some oranges

Non-count Nouns
some butter
some milk

Note:

- Count nouns are items we can count. They can be singular or plural.
- Use *a/an* with singular nouns. Use *some* with plural nouns.
- Non-count nouns are items we cannot count, like water and sugar. Non-count items are singular. Do not use *a* with non-count nouns. Use *some* with non-count nouns.

C Write *a*, *an*, or *some* for each item.

1. some salad dressing
2. ______ egg
3. ______ orange juice
4. ______ soda
5. ______ ice tray
6. ______ mayonnaise
7. ______ grapes
8. ______ apple
9. ______ waffle
10. ______ jam
11. ______ yogurt
12. ______ ice cream

CD 1 Track 44

D Listen to the conversation between the man and the woman. Circle the items they need at the store. Cross out the items they don't need.

milk
ice cream
eggs
cheese
salad dressing
soda
bottled water
butter
margarine
frozen vegetables

E Circle the correct word.

1. I put [salad dressing soda] on a salad.
2. I put [cream mayonnaise] in my coffee.
3. I like [yogurt jam] on bread.
4. I put [cake syrup] on waffles.
5. I drink [orange juice salad] for breakfast.
6. I like [pickles bacon] and eggs for breakfast.
7. I put [mayonnaise cheese] in tuna salad.
8. I'd like some [sour cream cake] for dessert.

Food to Go

A Write the word for each food item.

a bagel	a hot dog	a sandwich	~~beans~~
sushi	a muffin	french fries	egg rolls
a pizza	fish and chips	spaghetti	tacos

1. beans

2. ____________

3. ____________

4. ____________

5. ____________

6. ____________

7. ____________

8. ____________

9. ____________

10. ____________

11. ____________

12. ____________

B Cross out the food or drink that does not belong.

1. pizza	~~muffin~~	lasagna	spaghetti
2. tea	soda	french fries	coffee
3. bagel	muffin	doughnut	beans
4. ketchup	mustard	straw	salsa
5. pizza	egg roll	sushi	chicken teriyaki
6. taco	baked potato	burrito	tortilla

CD 1
Track 45

C Listen and write the number of each order under the correct picture.

a. ______________

b. ______________

c. ______________

d. ______________

e. ______________

f. ____1____

Grammar Connection: *I would like*

I would like I'd like	a hamburger. lasagna.

Note:

- *I would like* is a polite way to say *I want*.
- *I'd like* is the contraction for *I would like*. Use *I'd like* in conversation.

D Look at the food court in your dictionary. Write your order for each shop. Use *I'd like*.

1. Little Italy: I'd like a slice of pizza.
2. Bagels 'N' Burgers: I'd like ______________________________
3. Asian Express: ______________________________
4. Hot Salsa: ______________________________

E Complete each sentence with an item from your dictionary.

1. I like ______________________.
2. I don't like ______________________.
3. I put ______________________ on french fries.
4. I put ______________________ on a hamburger.
5. I put ______________________ on a baked potato.
6. ______________________ is a healthy choice.
7. ______________________ isn't a healthy choice.

Cooking

A What do you do with each kitchen item?

slice	stir	measure	bake
~~puree~~	grill	sauté	season

1. puree

2. ____________

3. ____________

4. ____________

5. ____________

6. ____________

7. ____________

8. ____________

Grammar Connection: Instructions

Slice **Dice** **Chop**	the onions.

Note:

- When you give instructions or directions, use the base form of the verb.

B Complete the instructions. Use one of the verbs in the word box.

1. Grill the steak.
2. ____________ at 350° for one hour.
3. ____________ two apples.
4. ____________ the flour, sugar, and milk.
5. ____________ the meat with salt and pepper.
6. ____________ the cheese.
7. ____________ a cookie sheet.
8. ____________ two eggs and a cup of water.

Mix
~~Grill~~
Peel
Bake
Add
Grate
Season
Grease

CD 1
Track 46

C Listen and complete the recipe.

Chop	Grease	Fold	~~Scramble~~	Cook
Grate	dice	Cook	Slice	Add

Omelette

4 eggs	3 ounces cheese
½ onion	3 ounces ham
½ green pepper	1 tablespoon butter

1. ____Scramble____ the eggs in a bowl.
2. ____________________ the onion and the pepper.
3. ____________________ the cheese.
4. ____________________ and ____________________ the ham.
5. ____________________ the frying pan with the butter.
6. ____________________ the eggs for a few minutes.
7. ____________________ the onion, pepper, cheese, and ham.
8. ____________________ the eggs for three more minutes.
9. ____________________ the omelette and serve immediately.

D Put the pictures in order from 1 to 9 to follow the recipe in Exercise C.

a. ____________

b. ____________

c. ____1____

d. ____________

e. ____________

f. ____________

g. ____________

h. ____________

i. ____________

Cooking Equipment

A **This woman is making vegetable soup. On the lines below, write the words for the equipment she is using.**

knife	cutting board	ladle	vegetable peeler	measuring cup
~~colander~~	can opener	pot	lid	measuring spoons

B **Match.**

f	1. mixing	a. sheet
____	2. food	b. spoon
____	3. cutting	c. board
____	4. cookie	d. thermometer
____	5. wooden	e. processor
____	6. meat	f. bowl
____	7. frying	g. cup
____	8. measuring	h. pan

Grammar Connection: Polite Requests

Please	pass me hand me give me bring me	the spatula.

Note:

- Start a polite request with *Please*.
- Use the base form of the verb.

C **Look at the cooking equipment in your dictionary. Complete these polite requests.**

1. I need to open a bottle. Please bring me the bottle opener.
2. I need to open a can. Please pass me the __________.
3. I need to fry eggs. Please hand me the __________.
4. I need to grate cheese. Please hand me the __________.
5. I need to measure milk. Please give me the __________.
6. I need to peel vegetables. Please __________.
7. I need to bake cookies. Please __________.

CD 1
Track 47

D **Two cooks are working together in a kitchen. Listen and complete the sentences.**

1. Please get the ladle.
2. I need a __________.
3. Do we have a __________?
4. Please hand me the __________.
5. Where's the __________?
6. I can't find the __________.
7. Do we have a __________?
8. Please give me the __________.
9. We need a __________.
10. Use the __________.

timer
peeler
~~ladle~~
steamer
spatula
knife
whisk
grater
wok
strainer

Measurements and Containers

A Write the word for each container.

a pot	a tube	a cup	~~a gallon~~
a pitcher	a jar	a carton	a basket

1. a gallon

2. ______

3. ______

4. ______

5. ______

6. ______

7. ______

8. ______

B Look in your dictionary. How many of each do you see in the picture?

1. bags of potatoes 2
2. boxes of strawberries ____
3. six-packs of soda ____
4. bottles of olive oil ____
5. pieces of cake ____
6. containers of yogurt ____
7. baskets of apples ____
8. cups of coffee ____
9. bouquets of flowers ____
10. loaves of bread ____

C Circle the two items you can put in each container.

1. a crate of . . .	(a.) melons	b. eggs	(c.) apples
2. a pot of . . .	a. tea	b. coffee	c. bread
3. a pitcher of . . .	a. lemonade	b. strawberries	c. iced tea
4. a bag of . . .	a. cake	b. cherries	c. apples
5. a tube of . . .	a. toothpaste	b. hand cream	c. eggs

Grammar Connection: Count and Non-count Nouns with Containers

Non-count Nouns
some coffee
some milk
some honey
some yogurt

Count Nouns
a cup of coffee
a gallon of milk
a jar of honey
a container of yogurt

Note:

- Non-count items are items we cannot count, like water and sugar. Non-count items are singular.
- We often put non-count items in a container. The container can be singular or plural.

D Each of these items is a non-count noun. Put each item in a container.

Non-count Nouns	Count Nouns
1. some soup	*a can of soup*
2. some cereal	______
3. some mayonnaise	______
4. some apple juice	______
5. some sugar	______
6. some bread	______
7. some tuna	______

CD 1
Track 48

E Listen and write the number of each statement or question under the correct item.

a. ______

b. ______

c. ______

d. ______

e. 1

f. ______

Supermarket

A In which supermarket section can you find each item?

frozen foods	dairy products	deli counter
bakery	produce	~~meats and poultry~~

1. meats and poultry 2. ______ 3. ______

4. ______ 5. ______ 6. ______

B Look at the supermarket in your dictionary. How many of each do you see?

1. checkout counters 4
2. cash registers ____
3. cashiers ____
4. baggers ____
5. shoppers ____
6. shopping carts ____
7. aisles ____
8. barcode scanners ____

C Complete the sentences with information about yourself.

1. My favorite supermarket is ______.
2. My supermarket has a very good ______ section.
3. I use a [shopping cart shopping basket].
4. The cashiers [use don't use] a barcode scanner.
5. There [are aren't] baggers in my supermarket.
6. I use [plastic bags paper bags] for my groceries.

Grammar Connection: *Where* Questions with *be*

Where is	the tuna?	**It's**	in the canned good section.
Where are	the paper towels?	**They're**	in the paper products section.

D **Complete the questions. Write the answers.**

1. Where is the yogurt? It's in the dairy section.
2. ____________ the bananas? They're in the produce section.
3. ____________ the soup? It's in the canned goods section
4. ____________ the pork chops? They're in the meats and poultry section.
5. ____________ the ice cream? It's in the frozen foods section.
6. ____________ the toilet paper? It's in the paper products section.
7. ____________ the muffins? They're in the bakery section.

E **Listen to the questions. Check the correct section of the supermarket.**

CD 1
Track 49

	Produce	Meats and Poultry	Dairy Products	Frozen Foods	Bakery	Deli Counter
1.	____	____	✓	____	____	____
2.	____	____	____	____	____	____
3.	____	____	____	____	____	____
4.	____	____	____	____	____	____
5.	____	____	____	____	____	____
6.	____	____	____	____	____	____
7.	____	____	____	____	____	____
8.	____	____	____	____	____	____

F **Match.**

____________	**1.** potato	**a.** scanner
____________	**2.** barcode	**b.** bar
____________	**3.** paper	**c.** register
____________	**4.** cash	**d.** bag
____________	**5.** candy	**e.** chips

Restaurant

A **Write the word for each restaurant item.**

a saucer	a saltshaker	a creamer	a pepper shaker
a napkin	~~a vase~~	a cup	a sugar bowl

1. a vase
2. ______
3. ______
4. ______

  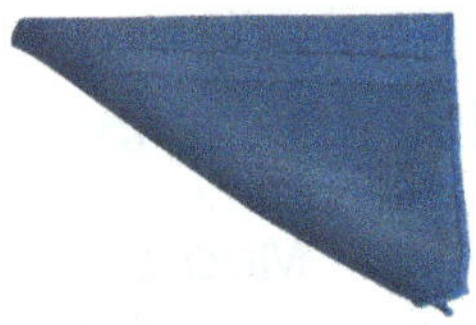 

5. ______
6. ______
7. ______
8. ______

B **Look at the restaurant in your dictionary. How many of each do you see?**

1. high chairs 1
2. vases ____
3. menus ____
4. appetizers ____
5. trays ____
6. servers ____
7. bowls ____
8. desserts ____

C **Look at the restaurant in your dictionary. Circle the correct word.**

1. The [chef dishwasher] is cooking in the kitchen.
2. The waiter is carrying a [tray vase].
3. The little boy is sitting in a [tablecloth high chair].
4. There's a [vase napkin] in the middle of the table.
5. Each table has a [menu tablecloth].
6. All the workers are wearing [diners aprons].
7. The man needs a [fork plate].

Grammar Connection: Polite Requests

May I please have	a napkin? a fork?

Note:

- Begin a polite request with *May I please*.
- Use the base form of the verb.

D Complete these polite requests.

1. May I please have a spoon?
2. ______________ a cup of coffee?
3. ______________ a knife?
4. ______________ a menu?
5. ______________ the check?
6. ______________ a napkin?

CD 1
Track 50

E Listen and draw each item in the correct place on this table.

F Imagine you are going out for dinner. Complete the sentences.

1. I am going to eat at ______________ (name of restaurant).
2. I am going to have ______________ for an appetizer.
3. I [am   am not] going to have the salad bar.
4. I am going to order ______________ for a main course.
5. I am going to have ______________ for dessert.
6. I am going to have a cup of [tea   coffee].
7. ______________ is going to pay the bill!

Order, Eat, Pay

A Complete the sentences.

Share	Spill	Light
Refill	~~Butter~~	Pour

1. Butter the bread.
2. ____________ the candle.
3. ____________ the water.

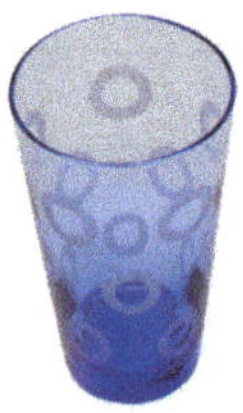

4. ____________ the coffee.
5. ____________ the glass.
6. ____________ the dessert.

B Who performs this action in a restaurant? Circle *Server* or *Customer*.

1. Make a reservation. Server (Customer)
2. Clear the table. Server Customer
3. Butter the bread. Server Customer
4. Drink. Server Customer
5. Refill the water. Server Customer
6. Signal the server. Server Customer
7. Light a candle. Server Customer
8. Set the table. Server Customer
9. Carry a tray. Server Customer
10. Leave a tip. Server Customer

CD 1
Track 51

C **Look at the restaurant in your dictionary. Listen to the statements and write the number of the server or customer.**

a. 7 d. ____ g. ____

b. ____ e. ____ h. ____

c. ____ f. ____ i. ____

Grammar Connection: Simple Past Tense with *When* and *After*

After the waitress **set** the table,	the first customers **sat** down.
When the food **was** ready,	the waiter **served** the meal.

Note:

- Most past tense verbs end in *d* or *ed*: share - shared order - ordered
- There are many irregular past tense verbs:

  make - made set - set take - took drink - drank
  eat - ate leave - left pay - paid
- Put the verbs in each part of the sentence in the past tense.

D **Match the parts of the sentence.**

f 1. After the family sat down, a. the waiter refilled it.

____ 2. After the family looked at the menus, b. they left a big tip.

____ 3. When the water glass was empty, c. the busboy cleared the table.

____ 4. When the little girl spilled her drink, d. the waiter took their order.

____ 5. After the children ate dinner, e. the waiter wiped the table.

____ 6. When the family paid the check, f. they looked at the menus.

____ 7. After the family left, g. they shared a piece of cake.

E **You are at a restaurant with a friend. Put the steps in order.**

____ Look at the menu. ____ Pay the check and leave a tip.

____ Order dinner. ____ Eat dinner.

____ Share a dessert. 1 Sit down at the table.

Word Study

You don't need to sit quietly when you study vocabulary. Act out new verbs. As you perform the action, say the word in English.

Clothes

A **Match the pictures and the sentences.**

a.

b.

c.

d.

1. He is wearing a T-shirt. __c__
2. He is wearing a suit. ____
3. He is wearing blue jeans. ____
4. He is wearing a jacket. ____
5. He is wearing a tie. ____
6. He is wearing a black shirt. ____
7. He is wearing a sweater. ____
8. He is wearing a white shirt. ____
9. He is wearing gray pants. ____
10. He is wearing shorts. ____

B **Write the word in the correct group.**

a sports jacket	a dress	a tie	~~a business suit~~
a gown	a tuxedo	a blouse	a skirt

Men's Clothes	Women's Clothes
a business suit	____
____	____
____	____
____	____

Grammar Connection: Present Progressive Tense – Third Person Singular

He	is wearing	a suit and a tie.
She	is wearing	a skirt and a blouse.

Note:

- The present progressive tense tells about an action that is happening now.

C Describe what each person is wearing.

Ali Bonnie Cara Dana Ed

1. Ali is wearing overalls and a T-shirt.
2. Bonnie ______.
3. Cara ______.
4. Dana ______.
5. Ed ______.

D Look at the picture above and listen to each statement. Circle *True* or *False*.

CD 1 Track 52

1.	(True)	False	6.	True	False
2.	True	False	7.	True	False
3.	True	False	8.	True	False
4.	True	False	9.	True	False
5.	True	False	10.	True	False

E What clothes do you wear?

To school: ______

To a party: ______

To work: ______

To exercise: ______

Sleepwear, Underwear, and Swimwear

A Write the word for each sleepwear, underwear, or swimwear item.

a blanket sleeper	~~slippers~~	a bathrobe	a camisole
a bathing suit	socks	a bikini	flip flops

1. slippers

2. ______

3. ______

4. ______

5. ______

6. ______

7. ______

8. ______

B Who wears it? Check *Man*, *Woman*, or *Both*.

	Man	Woman	Both
slip	___	✓	___
swimming trunks	___	___	___
pajamas	___	___	___
pantyhose	___	___	___
socks	___	___	___
stockings	___	___	___
slippers	___	___	___
leotard	___	___	___
undershirt	___	___	___

CD 1
Track 53

C **Look in your dictionary and listen to each statement. Write the number of the item you hear.**

a. 24 d. ____ g. ____

b. ____ e. ____ h. ____

c. ____ f. ____ i. ____

Grammar Connection: *How much* Questions with *be*

How much	**is**	**this** bathrobe?	**It's** $29.00.
How much	**are**	**these** slippers?	**They're** $11.00.

D **Complete the questions with *is this* or *are these*.**

1. How much are these flip flops? They're $7.00.
2. How much ____________ undershirt? It's $6.50.
3. How much ____________ pajamas? They're $20.00
4. How much ____________ slip? It's $16.00.
5. How much ____________ swimsuit? It's $25.00.
6. How much ____________ boxers? They're $10.00.
7. How much ____________ socks? They're $5.00.
8. How much ____________ bikini? It's $29.00.
9. How much ____________ bathrobe? It's $27.00.
10. How much ____________ briefs? They're $6.00.

E **Match.**

c	**1.** long	**a.** shorts
____	**2.** tank	**b.** top
____	**3.** athletic	**c.** underwear
____	**4.** boxer	**d.** sleeper
____	**5.** blanket	**e.** supporter

Shoes and Accessories

A Write the word for each item.

a ring	gloves	a purse	an umbrella
a key chain	sunglasses	~~a briefcase~~	a wallet

1. a briefcase

2. ____________

3. ____________

4. ____________

5. ____________

6. ____________

7. ____________

8. ____________

B Complete each sentence with a word from Exercise A.

1. When it is sunny, I wear sunglasses.
2. When it is raining, I take my ____________.
3. My car key is on my ____________.
4. I put my papers and books in my ____________.
5. I carry my money in my ____________.
6. A woman puts her wallet, keys, and makeup in her ____________.
7. I wear a ____________ on my finger.
8. When it is cold, I wear ____________ on my hands.

C Circle the shoes.

pumps	key chains	heels	belts
loafers	boots	clogs	wallets
sandals	purses	sneakers	hiking boots

Grammar Connection: Adverbs of Frequency

I **always** wear a belt.	always: 90% to 100%
I **often** wear a belt.	often: 70% to 90%
I **sometimes** wear a belt.	sometimes: 30% to 70%
I **never** wear a belt.	never: 0%

D **Complete the sentences about yourself with *always*, *often*, *sometimes*, or *never*.**

1. I ____________________ wear a watch.
2. I ____________________ wear a ring.
3. I ____________________ use an umbrella when it's raining.
4. I ____________________ wear sunglasses when it's sunny.
5. I ____________________ carry a wallet.
6. I ____________________ wear sandals.
7. I ____________________ carry a purse.
8. I ____________________ wear gloves when it's cold.
9. I ____________________ carry a briefcase.
10. I ____________________ wear a hat.

CD 1
Track 54

E **Listen to each conversation. Write the number of the conversation under the correct picture.**

a. ____________

b. ____________

c. ____________

d. ____________

e. ____________

f. ___1___

g. ____________

h. ____________

Describing Clothes

A **Circle the clothing item you see in each picture.**

1. (cardigan sweater) / turtleneck sweater

2. wide tie / narrow tie

3. short-sleeved shirt / sleeveless shirt

4. V-neck sweater / turtleneck sweater

5. low heels / high heels

6. short skirt / long skirt

7. light jacket / heavy jacket

8. pleated skirt / straight skirt

B **Write the opposite.**

informal	wide	long-sleeved
light	high	~~flared~~

1. straight leg jeans ____flared____ jeans
2. narrow tie ____________ tie
3. formal clothes ____________ clothes
4. short-sleeved shirt ____________ shirt
5. low heels ____________ heels
6. heavy jacket ____________ jacket

Grammar Connection: *Who* Questions and Answers with *be*

Who is wearing a light jacket?	Jack **is**. Jack and Brian **are**. No one **is**.

C Look at the pictures and answer the questions.

Alexa **Bev** **Carlos** **Dennis** **Edgar**

1. Who is wearing baggy pants? *Carlos and Dennis are.*
2. Who is wearing a short skirt? ______________
3. Who is wearing a long-sleeved shirt? ______________
4. Who is wearing a heavy jacket? ______________
5. Who is wearing a turtleneck sweater? ______________
6. Who is wearing a short-sleeved shirt? ______________
7. Who is wearing straight leg jeans ______________
8. Who is wearing casual clothes? ______________
9. Who is wearing a wide tie? ______________

CD 1
Track 55

D Look at the people in Exercise C. Listen to each question and write the name of the correct person.

1. *Bev*
2. ______________
3. ______________
4. ______________
5. ______________
6. ______________ and ______________
7. ______________
8. ______________

Fabrics and Patterns

A What is the fabric?

leather	denim	nylon
cotton	~~silk~~	wool

1. silk

2. ______

3. ______

4. ______

5. ______

6. ______

B Which fabric is more common for each item?

1. jeans:	silk	(denim)
2. pajamas:	silk	corduroy
3. shoes:	nylon	leather
4. coat:	suede	lace
5. pants:	corduroy	cashmere
6. robe:	silk	suede
7. T-shirt:	cotton	leather
8. sweater:	denim	wool
9. tie:	silk	lace

Grammar Connection: Order of Adjectives

	Color	Fabric or Pattern	Item
She's wearing a	white	cotton	blouse.
He's wearing a	gray and blue	striped	sweater.

C Complete the sentences. Put the words in the correct order.

1. (boots / leather / black) She's wearing black leather boots.
2. (scarf / silk / yellow) You're wearing a ____________________.
3. (black / stockings / nylon) She's wearing ____________________.
4. (wool / brown / jacket) I'm wearing a ____________________.
5. (red / skirt / velvet) She's wearing a ____________________.
6. (red and white / tie / striped) He's wearing a ____________________.

D Write the patterns under the correct ties.

solid	print	polka dot	floral
paisley	~~checked~~	plaid	striped

a. checked

b. __________

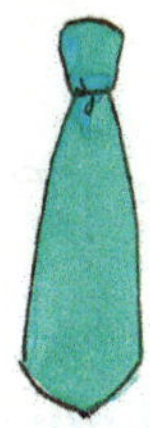

c. __________

d. __________

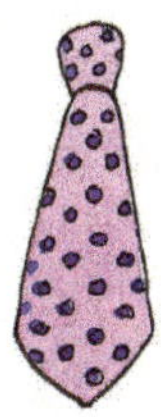

e. __________

f. __________

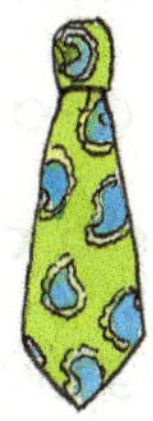

g. __________

h. __________

CD 1
Track 56

E Listen to each conversation and look at the ties in Exercise D. Write the letter of the correct tie.

1. f
2. ____
3. ____
4. ____
5. ____
6. ____
7. ____
8. ____

Buying, Wearing, and Caring for Clothes

A **What does each person need to do? Write the word for each action.**

Wash	Sew on	Roll up
Cut off	~~Zip~~	Button

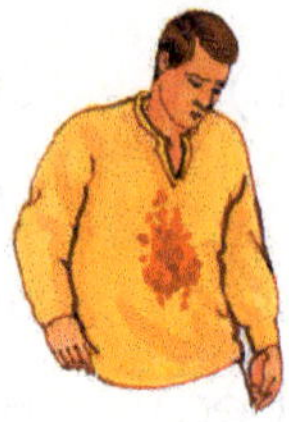

1. ___Zip___ the jacket. 2. __________ the shirt. 3. __________ the shirt.

4. __________ the button. 5. __________ the tag. 6. __________ the sleeves.

B **Look in your dictionary. Write the number of the correct picture after each sentence.**

1. The woman is looking for a jacket. __2__
2. She is trying on a jacket. ____
3. She is buying a jacket. ____
4. She is zipping the jacket. ____
5. She is buckling the belt. ____
6. She is unbuttoning the jacket. ____
7. She is taking off the jacket. ____
8. She is drying the jacket. ____
9. She is mending the jacket. ____
10. She is hanging up the jacket. ____

Grammar Connection: Possessive Adjectives

I am ironing **my** shirt.
You ironing **your** shirt.
He is ironing **his** shirt.
She is ironing **her** shirt.
We are ironing **our** shirts.
They are ironing **their** shirts.

C Complete the sentences.

1. She's putting on ___her___ jacket.
2. He's unbuckling __________ belt.
3. They're putting on __________ shoes.
4. I'm taking off __________ sweater.
5. He's hanging up __________ coat.
6. She's unzipping __________ dress.
7. I'm buttoning __________ shirt.
8. We're taking off __________ shoes.
9. They're washing __________ clothes.
10. He's mending __________ jacket.

D Listen and write the word or phrase you hear.

CD 1
Track 58

1. Mom, can we ___go shopping___?
2. Dad, can I __________ this shirt?
3. Mom, can you __________ my jacket?
4. Dad, can I __________ these jeans?
5. Mom, can you __________ my pants?
6. Dad, can you __________ my jacket?
7. Mom, can you __________ my button?
8. Dad, can you __________ my shirt?

buy
iron
wash
try on
~~go shopping~~
mend
unzip
sew on

Sewing and Laundry

A Write the word for these sewing items.

a safety pin	a thimble	a tape measure	a button
a pin cushion	a needle	a sewing machine	~~thread~~

1. thread

2. ______

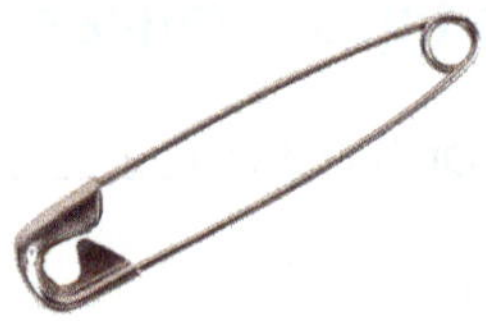
3. ______

4. ______

5. ______

6. ______

7. ______

8. ______

B You want to make a skirt shorter. Circle the items you need.

tape measure	pins	needle
button	pair of scissors	hanger
thread	zipper	thimble

C Match.

e	1. laundry	a. board
____	2. fabric	b. machine
____	3. laundry	c. softener
____	4. ironing	d. basket
____	5. washing	e. detergent

Grammar Connection: Present Simple Tense – *has / doesn't have*

The shirt **has** a collar.
The shirt **doesn't have** long sleeves.

D Look at the pictures. Complete the sentences with *has* or *doesn't have.*

1. The shirt ___has___ buttons.
2. The shirt ________ a collar.
3. The shirt ________ zipper.
4. The shirt ________ pockets.
5. The shirt ________ long sleeves.
6. The dress ________ a collar.
7. The dress ________ sleeves.
8. The dress ________ buttons.
9. The dress ________ a zipper.
10. The dress ________ a pocket.

CD 1
Track 58

E Charles does the laundry on Saturday morning. Listen and put the steps you hear in order.

____ Turn on the washing machine.
____ Put the dry clothes in the laundry basket.
____ Put the fabric softener in the cup.
____ Put the wet clothes in the dryer and turn it on.
____ Add the laundry detergent and bleach.
__1__ Separate the dark clothes and the light clothes.
____ Put the clothes in the washing machine.

Word Study

Try not to translate every new word. Instead, when you learn a new word, try to see a picture of it in your mind.

Vehicles and Traffic Signs

A **Look at the traffic signs in your dictionary. Write the names of six signs you pass on your way to school or work.**

1. ____________________
2. ____________________
3. ____________________
4. ____________________
5. ____________________
6. ____________________

Grammar Connection: Modals – *must* and *must not*

You **must stop** at a red light.
You **must not go through** a red light.

Note:

- Use *must* to explain rules, policies, and regulations.
- Use *must not* to show that an action is not permitted.

B **Look at the road signs. Complete each sentence with *must* or *must not*.**

1. You ____must not____ pass.

2. You ____________________ stop for pedestrians.

3. You ____________________ enter.

4. You ____________________ turn left.

5. You ____________________ yield to other cars.

6. You ____________________ drive slowly in a school zone.

CD 2
Track 1

C Listen and complete each sentence.

school bus	convertible	minivan	pickup
compact car	tractor trailer	~~SUV~~	tow truck
	motorcycle	RV	

1. My cousin lives in the mountains. He drives an ____SUV____.
2. My mother drives her ____________ with the top down.
3. My father works at a gas station. He drives a ____________.
4. My grandparents like to travel in their ____________.
5. My cousin has a farm. He needs a ____________.
6. My aunt works for a school. She drives a ____________.
7. My girlfriend wears a helmet when she rides her ____________.
8. My sister has three children. She loves her ____________.
9. My brother makes large deliveries. He drives a ____________.
10. My friend drives to work in his ____________.

D Match the vehicle and its use.

__d__	1. It makes large deliveries.	a. an ambulance
____	2. It picks up garbage.	b. an RV
____	3. It goes to fires.	c. a garbage truck
____	4. It takes people to the hospital.	d. a tractor trailer
____	5. It takes children to school.	e. a tow truck
____	6. It can have a bedroom and a bathroom.	f. a fire engine
____	7. It takes broken cars to a garage.	g. a school bus

E Circle each vehicle that you have ridden in.

a school bus	a minivan	a limo	an SUV
a convertible	a pickup truck	an ambulance	a motorcycle
an RV	a tractor trailer	a tow truck	a fire engine

Parts of a Car

A Write the words for the parts of this car.

~~windshield~~	trunk	hood	tire
fender	bumper	headlight	turn signal

B Match.

c	1. steering	a.	wiper
____	2. brake	b.	brake
____	3. windshield	c.	wheel
____	4. glove	d.	compartment
____	5. emergency	e.	mirror
____	6. rearview	f.	pedal

C Circle the correct word.

1. You want to make a turn. Use the [headlights   turn signal].
2. It is raining hard. Turn on the [windshield wipers   horn].
3. You want to check the oil. Open the [hood   trunk].
4. You want to stop. Step on the [accelerator   brake].
5. You want to start the car. Put the key in the [ignition   radiator].
6. You park on a hill. Put on the [emergency brake   engine].
7. You want to go faster. Step on the [brake   accelerator].
8. You are driving to school. Get in the car and put on your [seat belt   clutch].

Grammar Connection: Simple Present Tense Negative

The headlight **doesn't work**. The seat belt **doesn't work.**	The headlights **don't work**. The seat belts **don't work**.

Note:

- With *It*, use *doesn't* (*does not*) and the base form of the verb.
- With *They*, use *don't* (*do not*) and the base form of the verb.

D **Describe the car problems. Complete each sentence with *doesn't work* or *don't work*.**

1. The seat belt doesn't work.
2. The brake lights __________.
3. The oil gauge __________.
4. The heater __________.
5. The windshield wipers __________.
6. The speedometer __________.
7. The horn __________.
8. The turn signal __________.
9. The air bags __________.
10. The taillights __________.

CD 2
Track 2

E **Listen to each car problem. Circle the part of the car you hear.**

	a.	b.	c.
1.	**a.** accelerator	(**b.**) air conditioning	**c.** air bag
2.	**a.** taillight	**b.** turn signal	**c.** rearview mirror
3.	**a.** headlight	**b.** turn signal	**c.** brake light
4.	**a.** heater	**b.** horn	**c.** headlight
5.	**a.** battery	**b.** brake pedal	**c.** radiator
6.	**a.** windshield wipers	**b.** rearview mirror	**c.** glove compartment
7.	**a.** steering wheel	**b.** speedometer	**c.** accelerator
8.	**a.** ignition	**b.** gas gauge	**c.** oil gauge
9.	**a.** tire	**b.** trunk	**c.** taillight
10.	**a.** radio	**b.** rearview mirror	**c.** radiator

Road Trip

A **Look in your dictionary. Write the number of the correct picture.**

1. He put air in the tires. 18
2. They looked at a map. ____
3. They stopped at the stop sign. ____
4. She washed the windshield. ____
5. She passed a truck. ____
6. They changed the tire. ____
7. They arrived at their destination. ____

B **What do drivers do at a gas station? Check the correct answers.**

☑ **1.** Ask for directions.
☐ **2.** Pay a toll.
☐ **3.** Check the oil.
☐ **4.** Get gas.
☐ **5.** Pass a truck.
☐ **6.** Put air in the tires.
☐ **7.** Speed up.
☐ **8.** Wash the windshield.

C **What should a driver do in each situation?**

1. You are lost:	(**a.**) Ask for directions.	**b.** Speed up.
2. You have a flat tire:	**a.** Pull over.	**b.** Honk the horn.
3. You are getting off a toll road:	**a.** Speed up.	**b.** Pay the toll.
4. You have no gas:	**a.** Check the oil.	**b.** Get gas.
5. Your windshield is dirty:	**a.** Slow down.	**b.** Wash the windshield.
6. You see the exit you need:	**a.** Pass a truck.	**b.** Get off the highway.
7. You have an accident:	**a.** Pull over.	**b.** Look at a map.
8. It is getting dark:	**a.** Turn on the headlights.	**b.** Honk the horn.

Grammar Connection: Simple Past Tense Statements

He **checked** the oil.
She **asked** for directions.
They **parked** the car.

Note:

- Regular past tense verbs end in *d* or *ed*.
- There are many irregular verbs in English. For example:

drive – drove	get – got	have – had	leave – left
pay – paid	put – put	speed – sped	

D Complete the sentence with a past tense verb.

honked	got	checked	~~left~~
parked	slowed	changed	looked

1. After they put their bags in the car, they left.
2. When Jason sped up, he ________________ a ticket.
3. When the got lost, they ________________ at a map.
4. When they drove past construction, they ________________ down.
5. When Jason got gas, he ________________ the oil.
6. When Jason saw a cow on the road, he ________________ the horn.
7. When they got a flat tire, they ________________ it.
8. When they arrived at their friend's house, they ________________ the car.

CD 2
Track 3

E Last summer Tony and Maria went on vacation to the mountains. Listen and write the number of each sentence under the correct picture.

a. ________

b. ________

c. 1

d. ________

e. ________

f. ________

g. ________

h. ________

Airport

A **Write each word in the correct group.**

a ticket	~~a carry-on bag~~	immigration	baggage
a pilot	a boarding pass	a passenger	a flight attendant
a customs form	customs	a gate	

Luggage	People	Areas	Tickets and Forms
a carry-on bag	________	________	________
________	________	________	________
	________	________	________

B **Complete the sentences.**

seat	~~passengers~~	overhead compartment	economy class
aisle	seat belt	emergency exit	

There are two ____passengers____ in Row 14. They are not in first class. They are in ________________. Jacob is sitting in ________________ 14C. He has an ________________ seat. He's putting his carry-on bag in the ________________. Ava is sitting next to an ________________. She is wearing her ________________.

Grammar Connection: Present Progressive Tense – *Yes / No* Questions

Is she flying to India?	**Yes, she is.**	**No, she isn't.**
Are they flying to India?	**Yes, they are.**	**No, they aren't.**

C Answer the questions about the picture on page 124.

1. Are they sitting in first class? No, they aren't.
2. Are they sitting in Row 14? ____________
3. Is Ava sitting in an aisle seat? ____________
4. Is Ava wearing a seat belt? ____________
5. Is Jacob standing in the aisle? ____________
6. Is he putting his bag in the overhead compartment? ____________
7. Are Ava and Jacob talking together? ____________

D Match.

d	1. metal	a. bag
____	2. baggage	b. checkpoint
____	3. security	c. claim
____	4. carry-on	d. detector

____	1. boarding	a. exit
____	2. ticket	b. class
____	3. emergency	c. pass
____	4. first	d. counter

CD 2
Track 4

E Listen to each statement. Write the word you hear.

gate	flight attendant	emergency exits
immigration	~~photo ID~~	carry-on bag
seat belt	economy class	

1. photo ID
2. ____________
3. ____________
4. ____________
5. ____________
6. ____________
7. ____________
8. ____________

Taking a Flight

A Look at the pictures of the flight in your dictionary. Write the number of the correct picture after each sentence.

1. The woman is turning off her cell phone. 11
2. She is checking the monitors for her flight. ____
3. She is waiting at the gate. ____
4. She is stretching. ____
5. She is putting on her headphones. ____
6. She is asking for a pillow. ____
7. She is choosing a meal. ____
8. She is claiming her bag. ____
9. She is unfastening her seat belt. ____
10. She is going through security. ____

B Match the opposites.

f	1. Check your baggage.	a.	Put your tray up.
____	2. Board the plane.	b.	Land.
____	3. Turn off your cell phone.	c.	Unfasten your seat belt.
____	4. Fasten your seat belt.	d.	Get off the plane.
____	5. Turn on the overhead light.	e.	Turn on your cell phone.
____	6. Put your tray down.	f.	Claim your baggage.
____	7. Take off.	g.	Turn off the overhead light.

C Put each set of steps in order.

A		B		C	
____	Fasten your seat belt.	____	Get your boarding pass.	____	Get off the plane.
____	Find your seat.	____	Go through security.	____	Claim your bags.
1	Board the plane.	____	Check in.	____	Land.

Grammar Connection: Present Progressive Statements

He **is boarding** the plane.
She **is turning off** her cell phone.

D What is each person doing? Choose the correct verb and complete the sentence in the present progressive tense.

fasten	~~turn off~~	listen	stow
find	put on	stretch	turn on

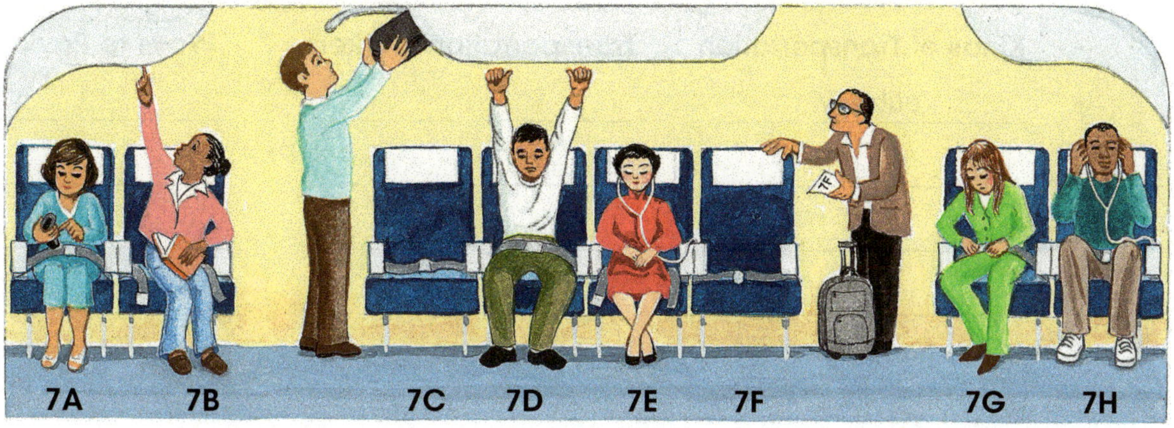

1. Seat 7A She ___is turning off___ her cell phone.
2. Seat 7B She ______________ the overhead light.
3. Seat 7C He ______________ his carry-on bag.
4. Seat 7D He ______________.
5. Seat 7E She ______________ to music.
6. Seat 7F He ______________ his seat.
7. Seat 7G She ______________ her seat belt.
8. Seat 7H He ______________ his headphones.

E Listen to each airport worker. What does the passenger need to do?

CD 2
Track 5

1. (a.) Show her photo ID. b. Check the monitors.
2. a. Wait at the gate. b. Get off the plane.
3. a. Fasten her seat belt. b. Find her seat.
4. a. Put on her headphones. b. Turn off her cell phone.
5. a. Get her boarding pass. b. Put her tray table down.
6. a. Claim her bags. b. Check in.

Public Transportation

A Write each word in the correct group.

~~subway~~	conductor	fare card	bus driver
token	taxi	train	taxi driver
ticket	bus	ferry	

Kinds of Transportation	Transportation Workers	Ways to Pay a Fare
subway	______	______
______	______	______
______	______	______
______		
______		

B Unscramble each word. What is the transportation word?

1. xati ______
2. rerfy ______
3. kntoe ______
4. srapt ______
5. ratkc ______
6. uleedsch ______
7. teerm ______
8. ilensttur ______

CD 2
Track 6

C Listen to these students talk about how they get to school. Complete the chart.

Name	How do you get to school?	How much is the fare?
1. Natalia	bus	$2.00
2. Adam	______	______
3. Lin	______	______
4. Salim	______	______
5. Francisco	______	______

Grammar Connection: Simple Present Tense Questions

How do you get to work?	I take the train.
What time do you catch the train?	At 7:30.
How much is the fare?	It's $8.00 round trip.
Where do you get the train?	At the Plainfield station.

D Complete the present tense questions.

1. How ___do you get___ to school?
   I take the bus.
2. Where ________________ the bus?
   At the corner of Pine and Broad.
3. What time ________________ the bus?
   At 8:35.
4. How much __________ the fare?
   $3.00 one way.

5. ___How do you get to work___?
   I take the subway.
6. Where ____________________?
   At 34th Street.
7. What time ____________________?
   About 6:30.
8. How much ____________________?
   It's $2.00. I use my fare card.

E Complete this information about public transportation in your area.

1. We [have   don't have] good public transportation in this area.
2. We can take the [subway   train   bus   ferry] in this area.
3. Public transportation is [cheap   expensive].
4. I [take the ________________ drive   walk] to school.
5. It costs $ __________ to take the ________________ from home to school.

Up, Over, Around

A **Start at the dot. Draw an arrow to show each of these directions.**

1. Go north. **2.** Go south. **3.** Go east. **4.** Go west.

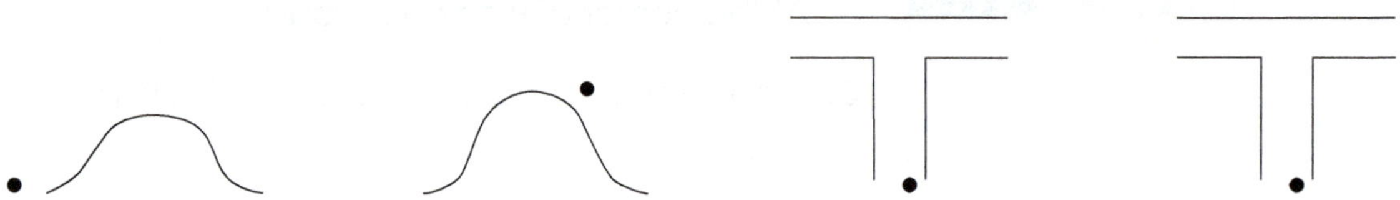

5. Go up the hill. **6.** Go down the hill. **7.** Go straight. Then turn right. **8.** Go straight. Then turn left.

B **Write the opposite of each sentence.**

Go into the tunnel.	Go up the hill.	~~Drive north.~~
Turn left.	Go over the bridge.	Take Route 22 east.

1. Drive south. Drive north.

2. Go down the hill. ____________________

3. Go out of the tunnel. ____________________

4. Take Route 22 west. ____________________

5. Turn right. ____________________

6. Go under the bridge. ____________________

Grammar Connection: Giving Directions – *First, Next, Then, After that*

Note:

- Use *First* to give the starting direction.
- Use *Next, Then,* and *After that* for some of the new steps in the directions.

CD 2
Track 7

C **Listen and complete the directions.**

through	over	along	past	across	around	into

1. First, I go ___over___ a bridge.
2. Then, I go __________ a park.
3. I go __________ a big church.
4. After that, I go __________ a river.
5. I go __________ a curve.
6. Then, I go __________ a tunnel.
7. I go __________ a railroad crossing.
8. I go __________ the parking lot.
9. I walk __________ the street.
10. I go __________ the school building.

D **Read the directions in Exercise C. Start at the house. Draw a line from the X to show the directions on the map below.**

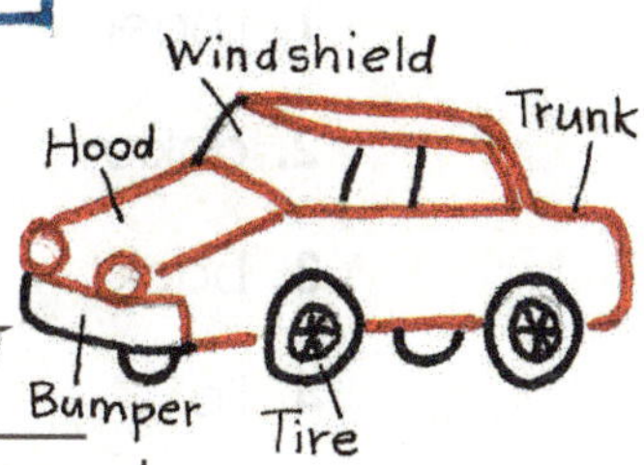

Word Study

Draw pictures of some of your new words. For example, draw some road signs. Or, draw a car and write the words for some of the parts.

The Human Body

A Write the parts of the body on the lines below.

hand	wrist	arm	chest
waist	hip	thigh	ankle
heel	neck	shoulder	toe
chin	~~nose~~	ear	back

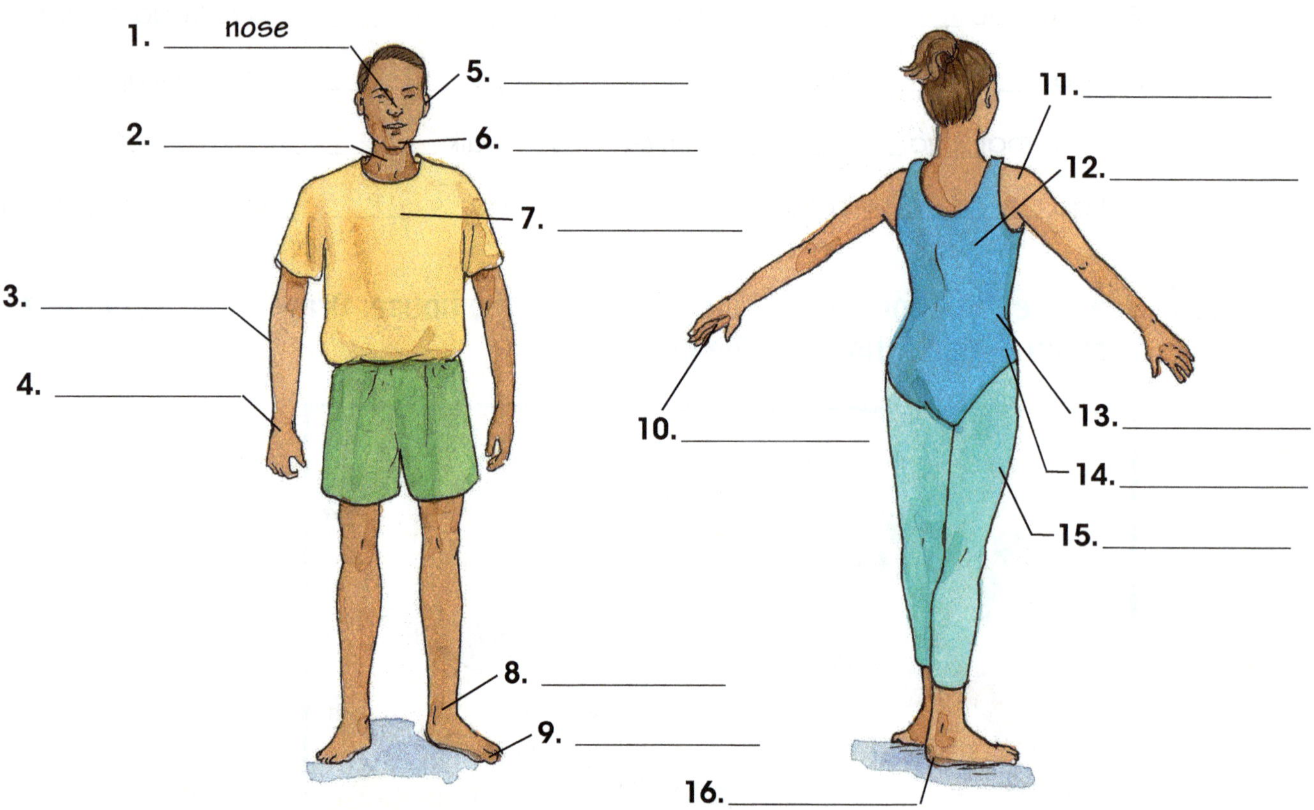

B How many do people have?

1. finger	10	**6.** waist	____	**11.** head	____
2. ankle	____	**7.** face	____	**12.** heart	____
3. back	____	**8.** fingernail	____	**13.** toe	____
4. lip	____	**9.** mouth	____	**14.** thumb	____
5. stomach	____	**10.** ear	____	**15.** neck	____

Grammar Connection: Possessive Adjectives

I - **My**
You - **Your**
He - **His**
She - **Her**
We - **Our**
They - **Their**

Note:

- Put a possessive adjective before a noun.
  My neck hurts.
- Possessive adjectives are the same with both singular and plural nouns.
  His shoulder hurts. **His** shoulders hurt.

C Complete the sentences with *my*, *his*, *her*, or *their*.

1. My father is at the doctor's. ___His___ shoulder hurts.
2. I am at the doctor's office. ______ back hurts.
3. My children are at the dentist. He's checking ______ teeth.
4. I am at the clinic. The doctor is checking ______ heart.
5. My mother is in pain. ______ leg hurts.
6. My brother is in the hospital. ______ stomach hurts a lot.
7. My sister doesn't feel well. ______ head hurts.

CD 2
Track 8

D Listen and complete these sentences. Then draw a line from each sentence to the correct picture.

1. Bend at the ______waist______.
2. Raise your ______________.
3. Stand on one ______________.
4. Touch your ______________.
5. Put your ______________ on your ______________.
6. Put your ______________ on your ______________.
7. Touch your ______________ to your ______________.

Illnesses, Injuries, Symptoms, and Disabilities

A **Look at the picture of the doctor's office in your dictionary. Write the number of the correct person.**

1. This girl is dizzy. 20
2. This child has lice in her hair. ____
3. This woman has asthma. ____
4. This boy has a bad sunburn. ____
5. This woman has a fever. ____
6. This boy has the mumps. ____
7. This man has a swollen ankle. ____
8. This woman has arthritis in her hands. ____

B **Match.**

c	**1.** swollen	**a.** pox
____	**2.** sore	**b.** sting
____	**3.** bee	**c.** ankle
____	**4.** bloody	**d.** nose
____	**5.** chicken	**e.** throat

CD 2 Track 9

C **Listen to each conversation. Circle the problem.**

1.	**a.** rash	**b.** bruise	**(c.)** flu
2.	**a.** stomachache	**b.** sore throat	**c.** swollen ankle
3.	**a.** acne	**b.** earache	**c.** arthritis
4.	**a.** bee sting	**b.** nauseous	**c.** dizzy
5.	**a.** flu	**b.** fever	**c.** bruise
6.	**a.** headache	**b.** backache	**c.** earache
7.	**a.** sprained wrist	**b.** swollen ankle	**c.** bee sting
8.	**a.** measles	**b.** sunburn	**c.** mumps
9.	**a.** stomachache	**b.** sore throat	**c.** sunburn
10.	**a.** blister	**b.** bloody nose	**c.** backache

Grammar Connection: Simple Present Tense - *have / has*

I You	**have**	a cold.
He She	**has**	

We They	**have**	colds.

D **Complete the statements with *have* or *has*. Then write the word(s) for each medical problem.**

allergies	a fever	a backache	the chicken pox
a cold	stomachaches	a cough	a sore throat

1. She has a cold.

2. He ______ ______________.

3. I ______ ______________.

4. They ______ ______________.

5. You ______ ______________.

6. They ______ ______________.

7. She ______ ______________.

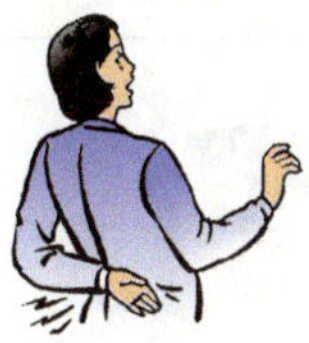

8. I ______ ______________.

Hurting and Healing

A **Look at the pictures in your dictionary. Write the number of the correct picture.**

1. A child is swallowing poison. 10
2. A man is drowning in the swimming pool. ____
3. A woman cut her finger with a knife. ____
4. A woman is unconscious. ____
5. A girl is having an allergic reaction. ____
6. A woman burned her hand. ____
7. A man's arm is bleeding. ____
8. A man is having a heart attack. ____
9. A man is choking. ____
10. A child is falling off a wall. ____

B **Complete the sentences about each picture.**

make	coughs	~~feels~~	sneezes	call

Donna (1) feels terrible. She (2)__________ and (3)__________ all the time. She is going to (4)__________ the doctor and (5)__________ an appointment.

Rest	Drink	feel	examining	Take

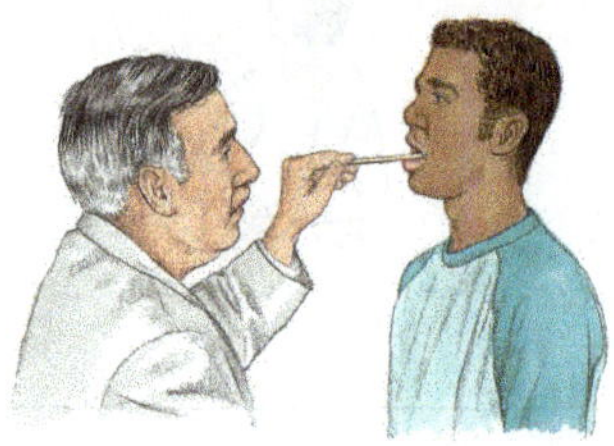

Adam is at the doctor's office. The doctor is (6)__________ him. The doctor is telling Adam, "You have the flu. (7)__________ in bed for three days. (8)__________ these pills. (9)__________ a lot of fluids. You will (10)__________ better in a few days."

Grammar Connection: Present Progressive Tense – Statements

I	am	bleeding.
He She	is	
They	are	

Note:

- Use the present progressive tense to talk about an action that is happening now.

C **Complete the statements with the verb in the present progressive tense. Then check the statements that are medical emergencies.**

☑ **1.** A man ___is choking___. (choke)

☐ **2.** A woman ______________. (cough)

☐ **3.** Two children ______________. (drown)

☐ **4.** I ______________ a heart attack. (have)

☐ **5.** A child ______________. (vomit)

☐ **6.** Some workers ______________ an allergic reaction. (have)

☐ **7.** I ______________ a lot. (bleed)

☐ **8.** A woman ______________. (sneeze)

D **This person has the flu. What advice do you have for her?**

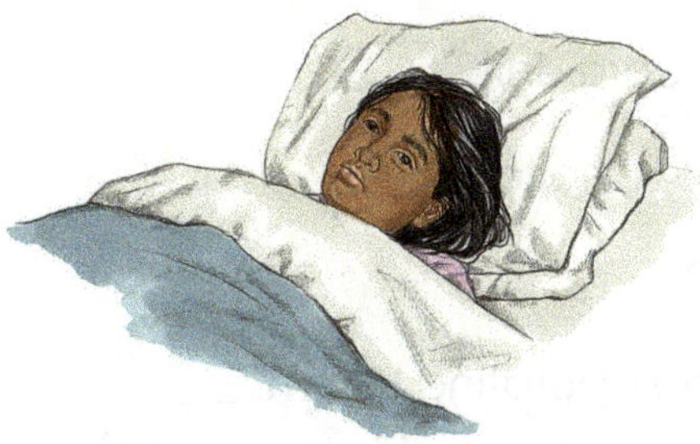

___Call the doctor.___

____

____

____

CD 2
Track 10

E **Listen to each emergency phone call. Circle the emergency.**

1. a. Her mother got an electric shock. **(b.)** Her mother is having a heart attack.

2. a. His son cut his arm. **b.** His son burned himself.

3. a. The driver is unconscious. **b.** The driver is in pain.

4. a. Her child is in shock. **b.** Her child swallowed poison.

5. a. A man overdosed on drugs. **b.** A man is drowning.

6. a. His daughter is bleeding. **b.** His daughter is having an allergic reaction.

7. a. Her friend overdosed on drugs. **b.** Her friend got an electric shock.

Hospital

A Write the word for each hospital item.

latex gloves	a stretcher	an ambulance	a hospital gown
~~a bedpan~~	a mask	an IV	a wheelchair

1. a bedpan

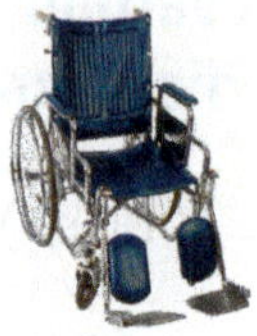

2. ________

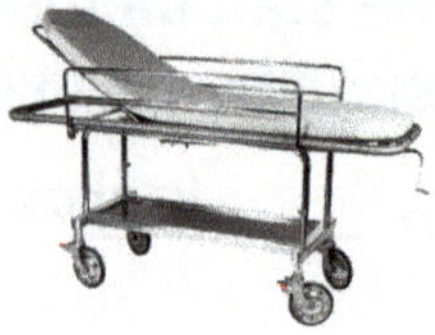

3. ________

4. ________

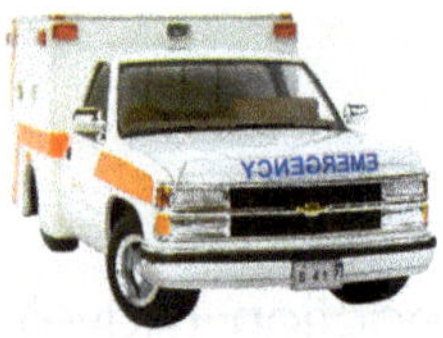

5. ________

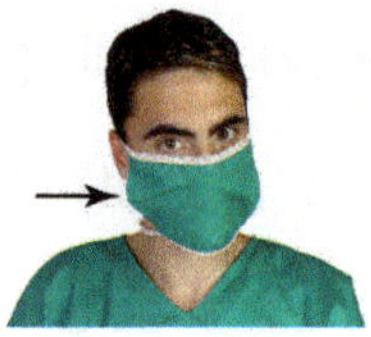

6. ________

7. ________

8. ________

B Look at the hospital in your dictionary. How many do you see?

1. How many patients are receiving blood? 1
2. How many patients are in the intensive care unit? ____
3. How many ambulances are outside the hospital? ____
4. How many patients are in wheelchairs? ____
5. How many doctors and nurses are in the operating room? ____
6. How many intravenous drips are there? ____

C Match to make true sentences.

f	1. A doctor	a.	performs operations.
____	2. A lab technician	b.	helps the nurses.
____	3. A surgeon	c.	gives anesthesia.
____	4. An anesthesiologist	d.	brings patients to the hospital.
____	5. An EMT	e.	takes blood.
____	6. An orderly	f.	checks patients.

Grammar Connection: Present Progressive Tense – Affirmative and Negative

I am visiting my friend. The doctor **is operating**. The nurses **are helping** the patient.	**I am not visiting** my friend. The doctor **isn't operating**. The nurses **aren't helping** the patient.

Note:
- Do not contract *am not.*
- The contraction for *is not* is *isn't.*
- The contraction for *are not* is *aren't.*

D Look at the hospital in your dictionary. Complete the statements with *am*, *am not*, *is*, *isn't*, *are*, or *aren't*.

1. The lab technician __isn't__ pushing a wheelchair.
2. The patient ________ pressing the call button.
3. The doctor ________ putting stitches in the patient's arm.
4. The nurses ________ performing the operation.
5. The nurses ________ helping the doctor.
6. I ________ bringing candy to my friend.
7. All the patients ________ wearing hospital gowns.
8. The orderly ________ pushing a patient in a wheelchair.
9. The paramedics ________ bringing a patient into the operating room.
10. The man's head ________ bleeding.

CD 2
Track 11

E Listen and complete the statements.

1. We need to take an ______X-ray______ of your arm.
2. Press the ____________________ if you need a nurse.
3. You need ten ____________________.
4. Your ____________________ is Friday at 7:00 A.M.
5. My brother is in the ____________________ unit.
6. The ____________________ will take you to your room.
7. Do you know how to do ____________________?
8. Can you bring me a ____________________?
9. I need to take some ____________________ from your arm.
10. She's an excellent ____________________.

stitches
blood
~~X-ray~~
CPR
bedpan
surgeon
call button
orderly
intensive care
operation

Medical Center

A Circle the people who can work in a medical center.

obstetrician	sling	receptionist	general practitioner
cardiologist	stethoscope	acupuncturist	braces
dentist	drill	psychologist	electrocardiogram
contacts	orthopedist	optometrist	pediatrician

B Circle the medical equipment that each specialist uses.

1. orthopedist:	**a.** sling	**b.** cast	**c.** filling
2. dentist:	**a.** drill	**b.** braces	**c.** contact lenses
3. optometrist:	**a.** cavity	**b.** eye chart	**c.** glasses

C Complete the sentences about each patient.

orthopedist	crutches	~~cast~~

Diana has a broken leg. Her leg is in a (1)_____cast_____. She needs (2)__________ to walk. She has an appointment with her (3)__________ next week.

tooth	dentist	filling	cavity

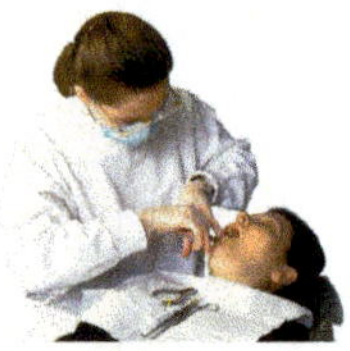

Marco is at the (4)__________. He has a (5)__________ in his (6)__________. The dentist is putting in a gold (7)__________.

obstetrician	sonogram	pregnant

Marta is seven months (8)__________. She is at the office of her (9)__________. The doctor is going to do a (10)__________ to check the baby.

eye chart	glasses	contacts	optometrist

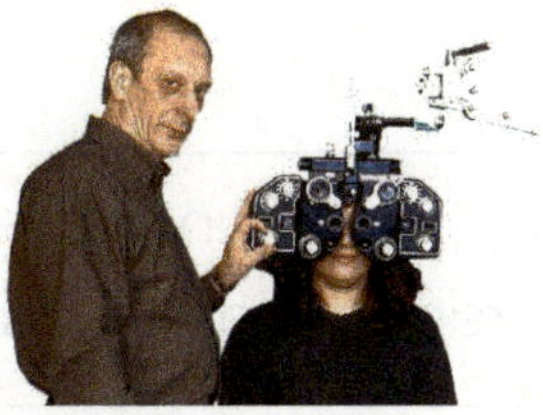

Ela is at the (11)________________. She is reading the (12)________________. At this time, Ela wears (13)________________. She doesn't like the glasses. She wants to try (14)________________.

Grammar Connection: Modal - *should*

You **should see** a psychologist.
You **should call** a psychologist.

Note:

- Use *should* to give advice or make a suggestion.

D Give each person advice. Use *should* in the answer.

1. I have a broken arm. You should see an orthopedist.
2. I have high blood pressure. ________________
3. My son has the chicken pox. ________________
4. My daughter needs braces. ________________
5. I think I'm pregnant. ________________
6. I can't see well when I read. ________________
7. I need my teeth cleaned. ________________

E What kind of doctor is each person talking to?

CD 2 Track 12

	a.	b.	c.
1.	a. a general practitioner	b. an obstetrician	(c.) a dentist
2.	a. a cardiologist	b. a psychiatrist	c. an optometrist
3.	a. an acupuncturist	b. an optometrist	c. an orthopedist
4.	a. a dentist	b. an obstetrician	c. a cardiologist
5.	a. a psychologist	b. an acupuncturist	c. a dentist
6.	a. a cardiologist	b. a pediatrician	c. an orthopedist
7.	a. a general practitioner	b. a dentist	c. an obstetrician
8.	a. a psychologist	b. a cardiologist	c. an orthopedist
9.	a. a dentist	b. a psychiatrist	c. an acupuncturist

Pharmacy

A **Write the word for each item.**

a cane	an elastic bandage	tweezers	an inhaler
a humidifier	a heating pad	~~a knee brace~~	a thermometer

1. a knee brace

2. ______________

3. ______________

4. ______________

5. ______________

6. ______________

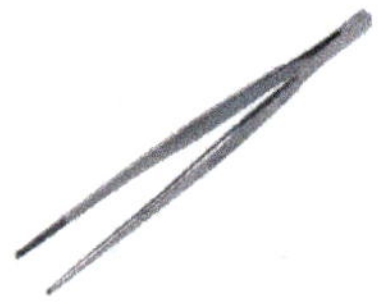

7. ______________

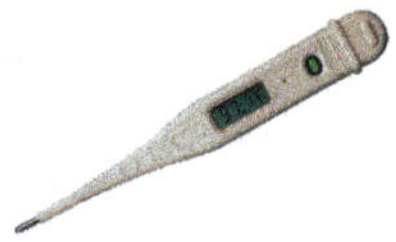

8. ______________

B **Look at the pharmacy in your dictionary. Complete this story about the customer in the pharmacy.**

elastic bandage	cane	prescription	~~pharmacy~~
pharmacist	capsules	knee brace	warning label

Randy fell and hurt his leg. He went to the doctor and he is now at the (1) pharmacy . He is speaking with the (2)______________. Randy is wearing a (3)______________ on his leg. He has an (4)______________ on his ankle. Randy is walking with a (5)______________. Randy has a (6)______________ from his doctor. The pharmacist is giving him a bottle of (7)______________. The medicine has a (8)______________. It says, "Do not drink alcohol while taking this medication."

Grammar Connection: Count and Non-count Nouns

Count Nouns	
Singular	**Plural**
an inhaler	some lozenges
a cane	some cough drops

Non-count Nouns
some medicine
some ointment

Note:

- Count nouns are items we can count. They can be singular or plural.
- Non-count nouns are items we cannot count. Non-count items are singular.

C **Read the medical problem. Complete the recommendation with *a*, *an*, or *some*.**

1. I have a cough. — **a.** Take ___some___ cough syrup.
2. I have a stomachache. — **b.** Try ________ antacid.
3. I have a headache. — **c.** Take ________ aspirin.
4. I have a sprained wrist. — **d.** Use ________ elastic bandage.
5. I have a stuffy nose. — **e.** You need ________ nasal decongestant.
6. I have dry eyes. — **f.** Take ________ eyedrops.
7. I have a sore throat. — **g.** Try ________ throat lozenges.
8. I have a backache. — **h.** Use ________ heating pad.

D **Check the items you have in your medicine cabinet. Write the brand you use.**

- ☐ **1.** aspirin ________
- ☐ **2.** antacid ________
- ☐ **3.** cough syrup ________
- ☐ **4.** vitamins ________
- ☐ **5.** throat lozenges ________
- ☐ **6.** nasal spray ________
- ☐ **7.** eyedrops ________

CD 2
Track 13

E **Listen to each conversation between a pharmacist and a customer. What does the pharmacist recommend?**

1. (**a.**) Try some throat lozenges. **b.** Try some nasal spray.
2. **a.** You need an inhaler. **b.** You need aspirin.
3. **a.** Use an elastic bandage. **b.** Use an antacid.
4. **a.** Try these eyedrops. **b.** Try an ice pack.
5. **a.** Go to the hospital. **b.** Go to the pharmacy.
6. **a.** You need a pharmacist. **b.** You need a prescription.
7. **a.** Try a humidifier. **b.** Try a heating pad.
8. **a.** Try a humidifier. **b.** Try hydrogen peroxide.

Soap, Comb, and Floss

A Complete the sentences.

1. You use __shampoo__ to wash your hair.
2. You use a ________________ to dry your hair.
3. You use a ________________ to curl your hair.
4. You use a ________________ to comb your hair.
5. You use a ________________ to brush your hair.
6. You use ________________ to wash your face.
7. You use a ________________ to shave your face.
8. You use a ________________ to brush your teeth.
9. You use a ________________ to cut your nails.

comb
nail clipper
curling iron
razor
toothbrush
brush
soap
~~shampoo~~
hair dryer

Grammar Connection: Adverbs of Frequency

I **always** use hair gel.
I **often** use hair gel.
I **sometimes** use hair gel.
I **never** use hair gel.

Note:
- Put the adverb of frequency before the verb.
- *Sometimes* can be used at the beginning or the end of a sentence.

B Put the words in each sentence in order.

put on / always / at the beach / I / sunscreen

1. I always put on sunscreen at the beach.

never / my father / aftershave / uses

2. ________________

wears / nail polish / my mother / often

3. ________________

always / my sister / wears / perfume

4. ________________

dental floss / sometimes / I / use

5. ________________

my hair dryer / my brother / often / uses

6. ________________

C Circle two products you can use on each part of the body.

1. teeth:	toothpaste (circled)	conditioner	dental floss (circled)
2. skin:	lotion	deodorant	shampoo
3. face (man):	mascara	shaving cream	aftershave
4. face (woman):	blush	hair spray	face powder
5. hair:	lipstick	hair gel	conditioner
6. nails:	perfume	nail polish	nail clipper

CD 2
Track 14

D Listen to the advertisements. Write the number of each advertisement under the correct picture.

Perfume

a. ________

Sunscreen

b. ________

Toothpaste

c. ________

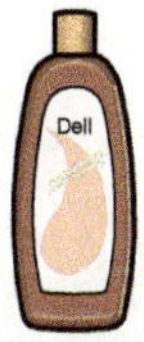

Shampoo

d. ___1___

Hair Gel

e. ________

Lotion

f. ________

Shaving Cream

g. ________

Deodorant

h. ________

Word Study

See, touch, and speak to help you learn new vocabulary. For example, pick up your toothbrush. Look at it. Feel it. Say the word (*toothbrush*). Put some toothpaste on the toothbrush. Say the word (*toothpaste*).

Jobs 1

A **Match the worker and the equipment.**

~~a firefighter~~	a gardener	a carpenter
a computer technician	an artist	an accountant

1. a firefighter

2. ______________

3. ______________

4. ______________

5. ______________

6. ______________

Grammar Connection: *What do you do?*

What do you do?	**I'm** a cashier.
What does your mother do?	**She's** a florist.
What does your father do?	**He's** a firefighter.

Note:

- To ask about someone's job, we say, "What do you do?"

B **Complete the sentences with an occupation from your dictionary.**

1. What does your mother do? She's a cashier.
2. What does your brother do? ______________.
3. What does your father do? ______________.
4. What does your sister do? ______________.

5. What does your uncle do? ______________________________.

6. What does your aunt do? ______________________________.

7. What do you do? ______________________________.

C Match the job and location.

b	1. cashier	a.	restaurant
____	2. assembler	b.	supermarket
____	3. housekeeper	c.	hospital
____	4. doctor	d.	factory
____	5. cook	e.	hotel
____	6. construction worker	f.	new building

D Listen and write the job you hear.

CD 2 Track 15

artist	actor
babysitter	janitor
health aide	editor
hairstylist	butcher
~~assembler~~	businesswoman

1. My uncle works in a factory. He's an assembler.
2. My cousin works in a school. He's a ______________________.
3. My aunt works for a big company. She's a ______________________.
4. My brother works in a nursing home. He's a ______________________.
5. My sister works in a studio. She's an ______________________.
6. My friend works for a book company. He's an ______________________.
7. My mother works in a beauty salon. She's a ______________________.
8. My father works in a supermarket. He's a ______________________.
9. My friend acts in movies. He's an ______________________.
10. My sister works for a family in our area. She's a ______________________.

Jobs 2

A Match the worker and the equipment.

a plumber	a locksmith	a photographer	a manicurist
a musician	~~a police officer~~	a scientist	a painter

1. a police officer

2. ______________

3. ______________

4. ______________

5. ______________

6. ______________

7. ______________

8. ______________

B Look at the jobs in your dictionary. Write one person who works in each location.

1. store: salesperson
2. hospital: ______________
3. office: ______________
4. museum: ______________
5. airport: ______________
6. school: ______________

C Match.

d	1. house	a. guide
____	2. security	b. agent
____	3. travel	c. therapist
____	4. tour	d. painter
____	5. physical	e. guard

Grammar Connection: Simple Present Tense - Third Person Singular

He She	**drives** a truck. **teaches.**

They	**drive** a truck. **teach.**

Note:

- For third person singular, add *s* to the verb.

D Circle the correct form of the verb.

1. A real estate agent [sell sells] houses.
2. A locksmith [install installs] locks.
3. Veterinarians [take takes] care of animals.
4. Soldiers [protect protects] their country.
5. A musician [play plays] a musical instrument.
6. Mechanics [repair repairs] cars.
7. A photographer [take takes] pictures.
8. Police officers [direct directs] traffic.

CD 2
Track 16

E Listen to the conversations. Circle the correct job.

1. **a.** scientist **b.** musician **c.** manicurist
2. **a.** lawyer **b.** photographer **c.** soldier
3. **a.** locksmith **b.** police officer **c.** nurse
4. **a.** travel agent **b.** receptionist **c.** realestate agent
5. **a.** veterinarian **b.** plumber **c.** physical therapist
6. **a.** plumber **b.** taxi driver **c.** tour guide
7. **a.** teacher **b.** reporter **c.** writer
8. **a.** pilot **b.** stockbroker **c.** salesperson

F Look at the jobs in your dictionary. Complete the sentences with your own ideas.

1. A ______________________ has an interesting job.
2. A ______________________ has a boring job.
3. A ______________________ needs a college education.
4. A ______________________ doesn't need a college education.
5. A ______________________ sometimes works at night.

Working

A **Look at the picture in your dictionary. Write the number of the correct worker.**

1. He is singing. 11
2. She is speaking. ____
3. He is driving. ____
4. He is repairing a bicycle. ____
5. She is calling in sick. ____
6. He is arresting someone. ____
7. They are making a decision. ____
8. She is making copies. ____
9. He is using a computer. ____
10. She is talking a message. ____

CD 2
Track 17

B **Listen and match each person with the correct action.**

d	**1.** He is	**a.** taking care of a child.
____	**2.** She is	**b.** acting in a movie.
____	**3.** He is	**c.** hiring a new worker.
____	**4.** She is	**d.** delivering a package.
____	**5.** He is	**e.** making copies.
____	**6.** She is	**f.** selling televisions.
____	**7.** They are	**g.** calling in sick.

Grammar Connection: Modal - *can*

I **can drive** a truck.
He **can cook** well.
They **can sing**.

Note:

- Use *can* to show ability.
- Use the base form of the verb after *can*.

C Complete the sentences with *can* and the correct verb.

schedule (crossed out)
sell
type
manage
speak
repair
plan
design

1. A receptionist can schedule appointments.
2. A mechanic ______________ a car.
3. An architect ______________ a building.
4. A travel agent ______________ a vacation.
5. A businessman ______________ an office.
6. A realtor ______________ house.
7. A secretary ______________ well.
8. An actress ______________ well.

D Read the statements about this office. Circle *T* if the statement is true. Circle *F* if the statement is false.

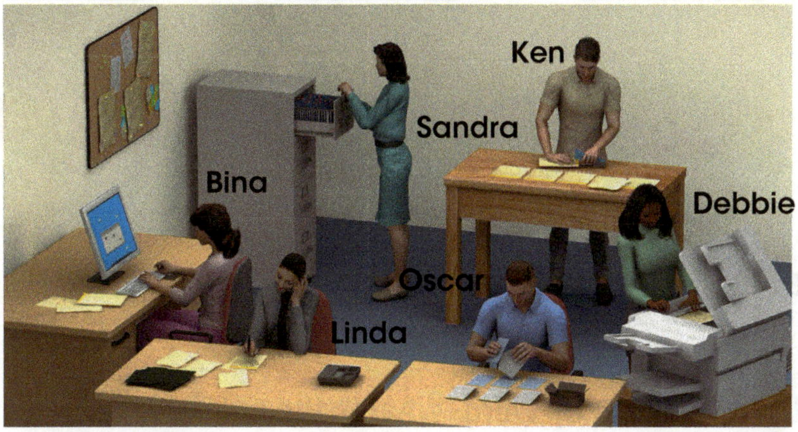

1.	Linda is taking a message.	(T)	F	6.	Bina is using a computer.	T	F
2.	Linda is hiring a new worker.	T	F	7.	Ken is designing a house.	T	F
3.	Oscar is opening mail.	T	F	8.	Ken is stapling papers.	T	F
4.	Debbie is making copies.	T	F	9.	Sandra is filing papers.	T	F
5.	Debbie is calling in sick.	T	F	10.	Sandra is making copies.	T	F

E Answer these questions about your job skills. Circle your answers.

1.	Can you cook well?	Yes, I can.	No, I can't.
2.	Can you take messages in English?	Yes, I can.	No, I can't.
3.	Can you drive a bus?	Yes, I can.	No, I can't.
4.	Can you repair a car?	Yes, I can.	No, I can't.
5.	Can you sing well?	Yes, I can.	No, I can't.
6.	Can you use a computer?	Yes, I can.	No, I can't.
7.	Can you type?	Yes, I can.	No, I can't.

Farm

A Write the word for each farm animal.

a turkey	a cow	a rabbit	a horse
a donkey	a rooster	a goat	~~a sheep~~

1. a sheep
2. ____________
3. ____________
4. ____________

5. ____________
6. ____________
7. ____________
8. ____________

B Unscramble each word. What is the animal?

1. egoos goose
2. gdo ____________
3. rohes ____________
4. lulb ____________
5. kicehcn ____________
6. gpi ____________

C Circle the correct word.

1. Milk the [cow rabbit].
2. Plant the [corn silo].
3. Pick the [scarecrow apples].
4. Feed the [chickens barn].
5. Put the hay in the [farmhouse barn].
6. Drive the [tractor goat].
7. Don't go near the [hay bull].
8. The scarecrow is in the [field barn].
9. The corn is in the [silo crop].
10. The farmer is watering the [plow crops].

Grammar Connection: Present Continuous Tense vs Future Tense

Present Continuous Tense	Future Tense
The farmer **is driving** the tractor. The farmer **is planting** corn.	The farmer **is going to plant** corn. The farmer **is going to drive** the tractor.

Note:

- The present continuous tense tells about an action that is happening now.
- The future tense tells about an action in the future.

D **Read about each farm picture. Underline the verbs in the present continuous tense. Circle the verbs in the future tense.**

The farmer is sitting on the tractor. The tractor is pulling a plow. The farmer is going to plant corn in the field. Then, he is going to water the field. The farmhand is picking grapes in the vineyard. After that, he is going to pick applies in the orchard.

The farmer and the farmhand are in the barn. The farmer is milking the cow. After that, he is going to milk the goat. The farmhand is feeding the chickens and the rooster. Later, the farmhand is going to feed the pigs.

E **Listen and circle the animal you hear.**

CD 2
Track 18

1. **a.** a pig **b.** a horse
2. **a.** a chicken **b.** a rooster
3. **a.** a dog **b.** a donkey
4. **a.** a sheep **b.** a cat
5. **a.** a dog **b.** a goat
6. **a.** a horse **b.** a cow
7. **a.** a sheep **b.** a cat
8. **a.** a chicken **b.** a pig
9. **a.** a donkey **b.** a turkey
10. **a.** a dog **b.** a pig

Office

A **Match.**

_d_	**1.** supply	**a.**	sharpener
____	**2.** pencil	**b.**	notes
____	**3.** appointment	**c.**	band
____	**4.** sticky	**d.**	cabinet
____	**5.** rubber	**e.**	clip
____	**6.** hole	**f.**	book
____	**7.** paper	**g.**	punch

B **Circle the office items that use electricity.**

computer	hole punch	fax machine	label
telephone	paper shredder	binder	copy machine

C **Complete the sentences.**

1. We correct mistakes with _correction fluid_.
2. We make holes with a ____________________.
3. We sharpen a pencil with a ____________________.
4. We send a fax on a ____________________.
5. We write a company letter on ____________________.
6. We write a short note on a ____________________.
7. We keep supplies in a ____________________.
8. We add numbers on a ____________________.
9. We make copies on a ____________________.
10. We keep papers in a ____________________.
11. We keep many folders in a ____________________.
12. We write appointments in an ____________________.

pencil sharpener
copy machine
sticky note
supply cabinet
~~correction fluid~~
file cabinet
folder
letterhead
calculator
fax machine
appointment book
hole punch

Grammar Connection: Short Questions and Answers with *be*

Is the computer on the desk?	Yes, **it is.**	No, **it isn't.**
Are the files in the file cabinet?	Yes, **they are.**	No, **they aren't.**

D **Look at the picture in your dictionary. Answer the questions.**

1. Is the stapler next to the telephone? No, it isn't.
2. Is the fax machine between the binders and the desk? ____________
3. Are the pencils in the supply cabinet? ____________
4. Are the binders on the file cabinet? ____________
5. Is the tape between the stapler and the computer? ____________
6. Is the pencil sharpener in the supply cabinet? ____________
7. Is the paper shredder next to the desk? ____________
8. Are the folders on the desk? ____________

CD 2
Track 19

E **Listen to each question. Write the number of each question under the correct item.**

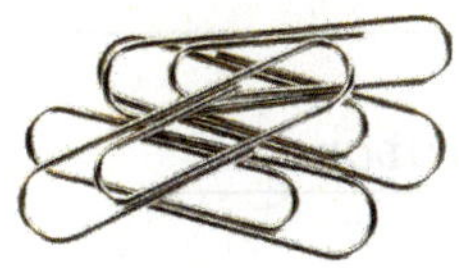

a. ____________

b. ____________

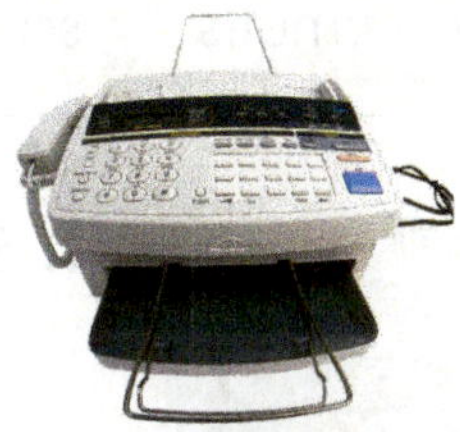

c. ____________

d. ____________

e. ____________

f. ____________

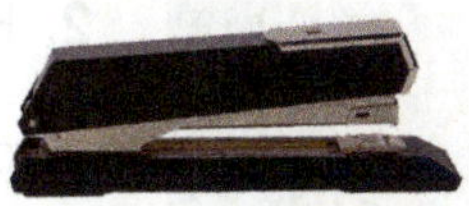

g. 1

h. ____________

i. ____________

j. ____________

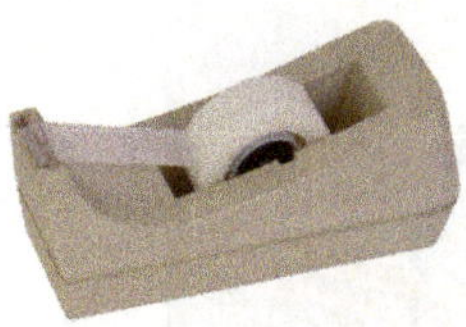

k. ____________

l. ____________

Factory

A **Look at the factory in your dictionary. How many do you see?**

1. How many packers are there? __1__
2. How many boxes are on the forklift? ____
3. How many workers are wearing hard hats? ____
4. How many workers are on the assembly line? ____
5. How many workers are wearing safety visors? ____
6. How many boxes are on the hand truck? ____
7. How many workers are wearing safety earmuffs? ____

B **What safety equipment is each person wearing? Complete the sentences.**

hairnet	safety boots	safety glasses	~~respirator~~
safety earmuffs	safety vest	hard hat	safety visor

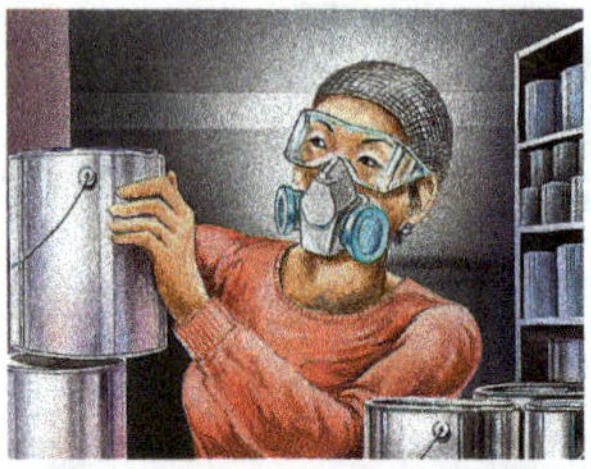

1. She is wearing a ______respirator______,
   a ____________________, and ____________________.

2. He is wearing a ____________________,
   a ____________________, and ____________________.

3. He's wearing a ____________________ and
   ____________________.

Grammar Connection: Modals – *has to / doesn't have to*

A packer **has to** wear safety boots.
A packer **doesn't have to** wear a safety vest.

Note:

- *Has to* shows that an action is necessary.
- *Doesn't have to* shows that an action is not necessary.
- Use the base form of the verb after *has to* and *doesn't have to.*

C **Look at the picture of the factory in your dictionary. Complete the sentences with *has to* or *doesn't have to.***

1. The designer doesn't have to wear a hard hat.
2. A factory worker ____________ use a time card.
3. An assembly line worker ____________ wear safety earmuffs.
4. The supervisor ____________ check the assembly line.
5. The machine operator ____________ take boxes to the loading dock.
6. The robot ____________ take a break.
7. The factory ____________ have a fire extinguisher.
8. The shipping clerk ____________ wear a respirator.

D **Match to make true sentences.**

a	1. A designer	a.	draws designs for a new item.
____	2. A packer	b.	sends the items to stores.
____	3. A supervisor	c.	watches the activity in the factory.
____	4. A shipping clerk	d.	puts the items in boxes.

CD 2
Track 20

E **Listen and circle the word you hear.**

	a.	b.
1.	(a.) hard hat	b. hairnet
2.	a. packers	b. parts
3.	a. assembly line	b. conveyor belt
4.	a. robot	b. time clock
5.	a. supervisor	b. shipping clerk
6.	a. safety glasses	b. safety goggles
7.	a. supervisor	b. respirator
8.	a. safety visor	b. safety vest

Hotel

A Write the answer to each question.

in the business center	in the fitness center	~~in the gift shop~~
with valet parking	in the ballroom	at the registration desk

1. Where can I buy souvenirs?

in the gift shop

2. Where can I make copies?

____

3. How do I park my car?

____

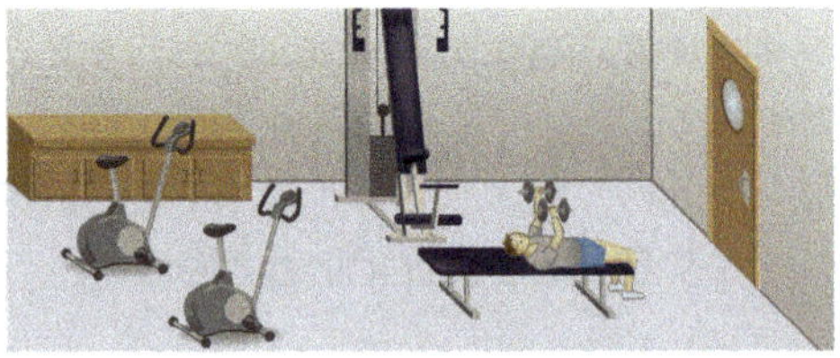

4. Where can I exercise?

____

5. Where can I check in?

____

6. Where is the party?

____

B Match.

c	1. valet	a. clerk
____	2. desk	b. pool
____	3. swimming	c. parking

____	1. revolving	a. room
____	2. single	b. door
____	3. room	c. service

Grammar Connection: Simple Present Tense - Questions and Answers

Does the hotel **have** valet parking?	Yes, it **does.**	No, it **doesn't.**
Does the hotel **have** a pool?	Yes, it **does.**	No, it **doesn't.**

C Complete the answers to the questions.

1. Does the hotel have a pool? Yes, it does.
2. Does the hotel have a fitness center? No, ________
3. Does the hotel have a gift shop? No, ________
4. Does the hotel have a business center? Yes, ________
5. Does the hotel have a sauna? No, ________
6. Does the hotel have a concierge? No, ________
7. Does the hotel have a ballroom? Yes, ________
8. Does the hotel have a meeting room? No, ________

D Look at the hotel in your dictionary. Circle the correct word.

The Hilltop Hotel is very quiet this morning. No one is walking through the [revolving door suite]. No guests are standing in the [concierge lobby]. No one is checking in at the [registration desk sauna]. The [lobby concierge] is not giving information to any guests. The bellhop is pushing an empty [pool luggage cart]. No one is going up the [gift shop escalator]. No one is using the computers in the [fitness center business center]. Only two men are working in the [meeting room ballroom]. Most of the rooms are empty. Where is everyone?

CD 2
Track 21

E Listen to each hotel guest. Where is the guest? Circle the correct place in the hotel.

1. **a.** escalator **b.** gift shop
2. **a.** registration desk **b.** escalator
3. **a.** sauna **b.** ballroom
4. **a.** valet parking **b.** bellhop
5. **a.** gift shop **b.** business center
6. **a.** lobby **b.** fitness center
7. **a.** escalator **b.** meeting room
8. **a.** sauna **b.** room service

Tools and Supplies 1

A Write the words for the tools and supplies you see in the picture.

router	drill	~~level~~
hammer	power sander	vise
ruler	file	extension cord

1. level
2. ______
3. ______
4. ______
5. ______
6. ______
7. ______
8. ______
9. ______

CD 2
Track 22

B Look at the picture in Exercise A. Listen to each statement and circle *True* or *False.*

1.	(True)	False	5. True	False	9.	True	False
2.	True	False	6. True	False	10.	True	False
3.	True	False	7. True	False	11.	True	False
4.	True	False	8. True	False	12.	True	False

Grammar Connection: Simple Present Tense - *Yes/No* Questions

Do you have a screwdriver?	Yes, I **do.**
Do you have a power sander?	No, I **don't.**

C Answer these questions about the tools you have at home.

1. Do you have a hammer? ____________________
2. Do you have a screwdriver? ____________________
3. Do you have a wrench? ____________________
4. Do you have a level? ____________________
5. Do you have a drill? ____________________
6. Do you have a circular saw? ____________________
7. Do you have a handsaw? ____________________

D Which tool do you use with each item?

a flashlight	a power sander	a hammer
~~a screwdriver~~	a drill	a wrench

1. a screwdriver

2. ____________________

3. ____________________

4. ____________________

5. ____________________

6. ____________________

E Match.

c	1. extension	a. gun
____	2. caulking	b. belt
____	3. tool	c. cord

____	1. utility	a. saw
____	2. pipe	b. wrench
____	3. circular	c. knife

Tools and Supplies 2

A **Circle the tools and supplies the workers are using.**

tape measure	molding	drywall	rope
shingles	masking tape	chain	sandpaper
insulation	screws	padlock	scraper

B **Circle the correct word.**

1. Put [tile insulation] on the floor.
2. Put a [scraper hinge] on the door.
3. Use a [hook tape measure] to measure.
4. Put the paint in a [paint tray flashlight].
5. Use a [roller rope] to put paint on the wall.
6. Put [shingles masking tape] on the outside of a house.
7. Use [sandpaper insulation] to keep the house warm.
8. Put [steel wool batteries] in the flashlight.

Grammar Connection: *It / Them*

Where's **the hinge**?	I have **it**.
Where are **the screws**?	I have **them**.

C Complete the answers with *it* or *them*.

1. Where's the masking tape? I have ___it___.
2. Where are the nails? I have ________.
3. Where are the screws? I have ________.
4. Where is the paintbrush? I have ________.
5. Where is the lock? I have ________.
6. Where are the hooks? I have ________.
7. Where are the batteries? I have ________.
8. Where is the insulation? I have ________.

D Match.

_f_	**1.** tape	**a.** wool
___	**2.** masking	**b.** roller
___	**3.** paint	**c.** nut
___	**4.** steel	**d.** tape
___	**5.** wing	**e.** lumber
___	**6.** board	**f.** measure

CD 2
Track 23

E Listen and write the number of the sentence you hear under the correct picture.

a. ________

b. ________

c. ________

d. ________

e. ________

f. ___1___

Drill, Sand, Paint

A Match the picture and the action.

a

b

c

d

e

f

g

h

1. He sanded the wood. __d__
2. He painted the wall. ____
3. He welded the metal. ____
4. He cut the wood. ____
5. He hammered a nail. ____
6. He dug a trench. ____
7. He drilled a hole. ____
8. He measured the wood. ____

Grammar Connection: Simple Past Tense – Statements

I **sanded** the wood.
You **installed** the window.
We **dug** a hole.
He **plastered** the wall.
She **painted** the windows.
They **wired** the house.

Note:

- Regular past tense verbs end in *d* or *ed*.
- Many verbs are irregular in the past tense:

cut – cut   read – read   tear – tore   dig – dug

B Write the verb in the past tense.

1. I __climbed__ the ladder. (climb)
2. The workers ___________ a trench around the house. (dig)
3. They ___________ a new window in the kitchen. (install)
4. I ___________ my bedroom blue. (paint)
5. We ___________ down the old garage. (tear)
6. He carefully ___________ the blueprints. (read)
7. They ___________ the lumber into the house. (carry)
8. She ___________ the wood before she ___________ it. (measure / cut)

CD 2
Track 24

C Listen and circle the instructions you hear.

1. **a.** Put up the drywall. **(b.)** Plaster the drywall.
2. **a.** Wire the house. **b.** Weld the house.
3. **a.** Pull the wheelbarrow. **b.** Push the wheelbarrow.
4. **a.** Plaster the wall. **b.** Paint the wall.
5. **a.** Sand the wood. **b.** Saw the wood.
6. **a.** Pour the concrete. **b.** Put up the concrete.
7. **a.** Drill a hole. **b.** Dig a hole.
8. **a.** Put up the drywall. **b.** Tear down the drywall.

D What can you do? Circle your answers.

1. Can you read blueprints? Yes, I can. No, I can't.
2. Can you put up drywall? Yes, I can. No, I can't.
3. Can you paint a room? Yes, I can. No, I can't.
4. Can you wire a house? Yes, I can. No, I can't.
5. Can you install a window? Yes, I can. No, I can't.
6. Can you saw wood? Yes, I can. No, I can't.

Word Study

When you see a sign in English, read it and say the words. Each time you pass the sign, say the words. You will be able to learn many words and phrases, for example: Do Not Enter, Office Closed, Do Not Disturb.

Weather

A Read the temperature. Complete the information about the weather.

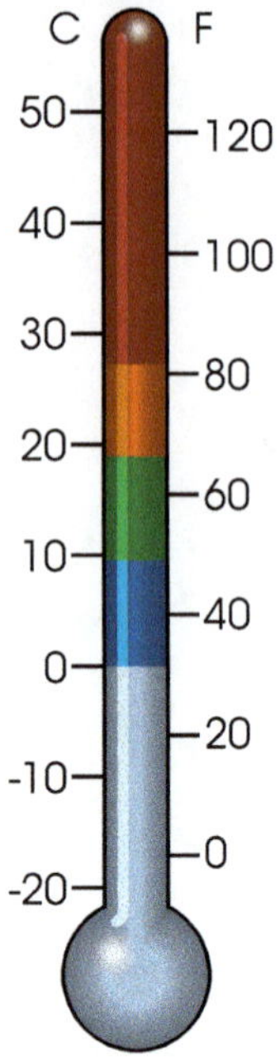

	Celsius	Fahrenheit	Weather
1.	4°	40°	It's cold.
2.	38°	100°	It's ______.
3.	-7°	20°	It's ______.
4.	24°	75°	It's ______.
5.	10°	50°	It's ______.
6.	-23°	-10°	It's ______.
7.	32°	90°	It's ______.

hot
warm
cool
cold
freezing

B Circle the correct word.

1. There are dark clouds in the sky. A [sun storm] is coming.
2. After a storm, you can sometimes see a [fog rainbow] in the sky.
3. We can't ski. There isn't any [rain snow].
4. It's difficult to see in the [fog sky].
5. Every [snowflake sun] is different.
6. Large [raindrops hailstones] can break a window.
7. Be careful. Don't fall on the [ice fog].
8. There is 10 inches of [wind snow] on the ground.

C Write about the weather in your area.

1. Yesterday it was ______.
2. Today it is ______.
3. Tomorrow it is going to be ______.

Grammar Connection: Future with *going to be*

It	is going to be	cold.
It	is going to be	cloudy.

D **Write the weather forecast for each picture. Use the future with *going to be*.**

1.  It is going to be sunny.

2.  ______________________________.

3.  ______________________________.

4.  ______________________________.

CD 2
Track 25

E **Listen to the weather report for the week. Draw the symbols to show the weather for each day. Then circle the word for the temperature.**

rain

snow

sun

wind

clouds

Monday	Tuesday	Wednesday	Thursday	Friday
 hot warm cool cold freezing	hot warm cool cold freezing	hot warm cool cold freezing	hot warm cool cold freezing	hot warm cool cold freezing

The Earth's Surface

A **Write the word for each feature on the map.**

river	valley	mountains	forest
bay	volcano	lake	~~ocean~~

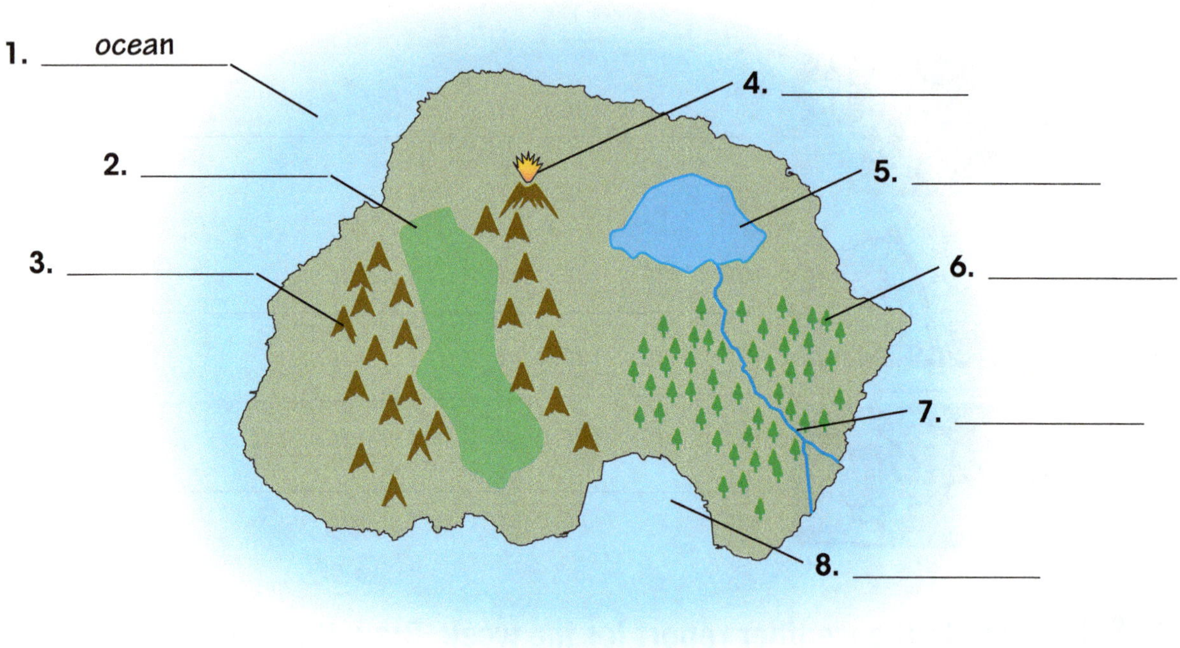

B **Look at the map in Exercise A and listen to each sentence. Circle *T* if the statement is true. Circle *F* if the statement is false.**

CD 2
Track 26

1. (T) F	**4.** T F	**7.** T F
2. T F	**5.** T F	**8.** T F
3. T F	**6.** T F	**9.** T F

C **Circle the features with water.**

(bay)	forest	mesa	ocean
plains	waterfall	stream	hill
river	lake	cave	canyon

Grammar Connection: Definitions

A lake is **a large body of fresh water.**
A valley is **a flat area between mountains.**

Note:
- A definition gives the meaning of a word.

D Complete the definitions.

peak
stream
plateau
~~ocean~~
forest
riverbank
glacier
desert

1. An ___ocean___ is a large body of salt water.
2. A ______________ is an area with many trees.
3. A ______________ is an area that gets little rainfall.
4. A ______________ is the top of a mountain.
5. A ______________ is a high, flat area.
6. A ______________ is a small river.
7. A ______________ is the area on the side of a river.
8. A ______________ is a river of ice.

E Match each feature with a famous example.

_b_	1. lake	a. Pacific
___	2. island	b. Superior
___	3. desert	c. Sahara
___	4. river	d. Niagara Falls
___	5. ocean	e. Cuba
___	6. waterfall	f. Amazon

F Complete with information about your country.

1. I'm from ______________ (country).
2. My country [is is not] on an ocean.
3. The largest lake in my country is ______________.
4. The tallest mountain is ______________.
5. The longest river is ______________.
6. The most beautiful waterfall is ______________.

Energy, Pollution, and Natural Disasters

A Write the word for each natural disaster.

a tornado	a blizzard	a forest fire
~~an earthquake~~	a flood	a volcanic eruption

1. an earthquake

2. ________

3. ________

4. ________

5. ________

6. ________

B Match.

b	1. air	a. waste
____	2. pesticide	b. pollution
____	3. oil	c. exhaust
____	4. automobile	d. poisoning
____	5. acid	e. spill
____	6. hazardous	f. rain

C Look in your dictionary. Circle the type of pollution each can produce.

1. cars:	water pollution	(automobile exhaust)
2. people on the street:	radiation	litter
3. factories:	air pollution	litter
4. household cleaners:	hazardous waste	oil spill
5. nuclear power plants:	pesticide poisoning	radiation

Grammar Connection: Past Tense of *be*

There **was** a tornado in Oklahoma last week.
There **were** three tornadoes in Texas last month.

D Complete the sentences with *was* or *were*.

1. There __________ a terrible earthquake in Haiti 2010.
2. There __________ bad floods in North Dakota a few years ago.
3. There __________ five hurricanes in the Caribbean last year.
4. There __________ a major tsunami in Japan in 2011.
5. There __________ several avalanches in Switzerland last year.
6. There __________ many tornadoes in the United States last year.
7. There __________ a blizzard in Colorado last winter.
8. There __________ a volcanic eruption in Mexico last year.
9. There __________ many forest fires in California last summer.
10. There __________ a mudslide on the mountain after the storm.

E Unscramble each word. Write the type of energy.

1. larso gneeyr ___*solar energy*___
2. dwin ____________________
3. antrula sag ____________________
4. lcoa ____________________
5. ilo ____________________
6. roeumptel ____________________

CD 2
Track 27

F Listen to each news report. Write the natural disaster you hear.

1. ___*floods*___
2. ____________________
3. ____________________
4. ____________________
5. ____________________
6. ____________________

blizzard
hurricane
forest fires
~~floods~~
avalanche
drought

The United States and Canada

A **Write the name of the state or province.**

Texas	Florida	Virginia	~~California~~
Nevada	Hawaii	Alaska	New York

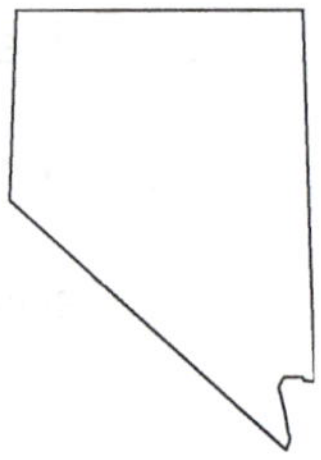

1. California
2. ____________
3. ____________
4. ____________

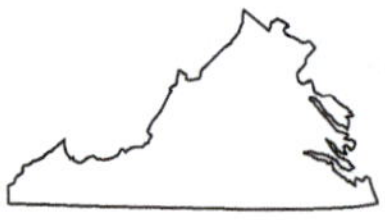

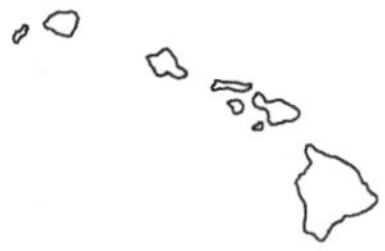

5. ____________
6. ____________
7. ____________
8. ____________

B **Look at the map in your dictionary. Circle *T* if the statement is true. Circle *F* if the statement is false.**

1. There are fifty states in the United States. (T) F
2. Washington, D.C. is the capital of the United States. T F
3. Canada has fifty provinces. T F
4. Canada is north of the United States. T F
5. Alaska is next to Yukon. T F
6. North Carolina is on the Atlantic Ocean. T F
7. Hawaii is in the Atlantic Ocean. T F
8. Texas is on the Pacific Ocean. T F
9. Santa Fe is the capital of New Mexico. T F

Grammar Connection: Locations on a Map

Kansas is in the Midwest. It is **north of** Oklahoma.
Florida is in the South. It is **south of** Georgia.

C **Look at the map in your dictionary. Complete the locations with *north of*, *east of*, *south of*, or *west of*.**

1. Ohio is in the Midwest. It is ___east of___ Indiana.
2. Oregon is on the West Coast. It is ______________ California.
3. North Carolina is in the South. It is ______________ Virginia.
4. New York is a Mid-Atlantic State. It is ______________ Pennsylvania.
5. New Mexico is in the Southwest. It is ______________ Texas.
6. Utah is a Rocky Mountain State. It is ______________ Nevada.
7. Connecticut is in New England. It is ______________ Massachusetts.
8. South Carolina is in the South. It is ______________ Georgia.

D **Look at the map in your dictionary. Complete the information about Canada.**

1. The capital of Canada is ___Ottawa___.
2. Canada is [north south] of the United States.
3. There are ______________ provinces in Canada.
4. There are ______________ provinces in Northern Canada.
5. ______________ is the largest province.
6. ______________ is the capital of Quebec.
7. ______________ is the capital of British Columbia.

CD 2
Track 28

E **Listen and write the name of the state you hear.**

Rhode Island	California	~~Alaska~~	Florida
Kansas	Colorado	Hawaii	Delaware

1. ___Alaska___
2. ______________
3. ______________
4. ______________
5. ______________
6. ______________
7. ______________
8. ______________

The World

A Look in your dictionary. Write the name of each continent on the world map.

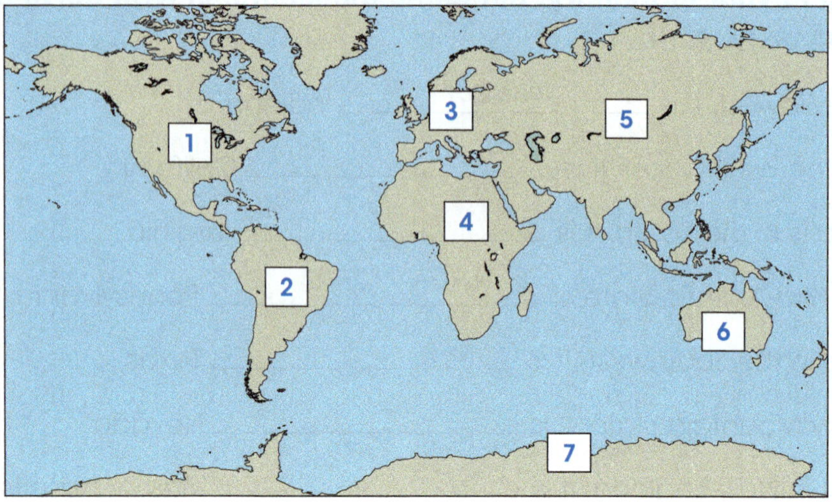

1. North America
2. ______
3. ______
4. ______
5. ______
6. ______
7. ______

B Look in your dictionary. Write the word for each part of the earth.

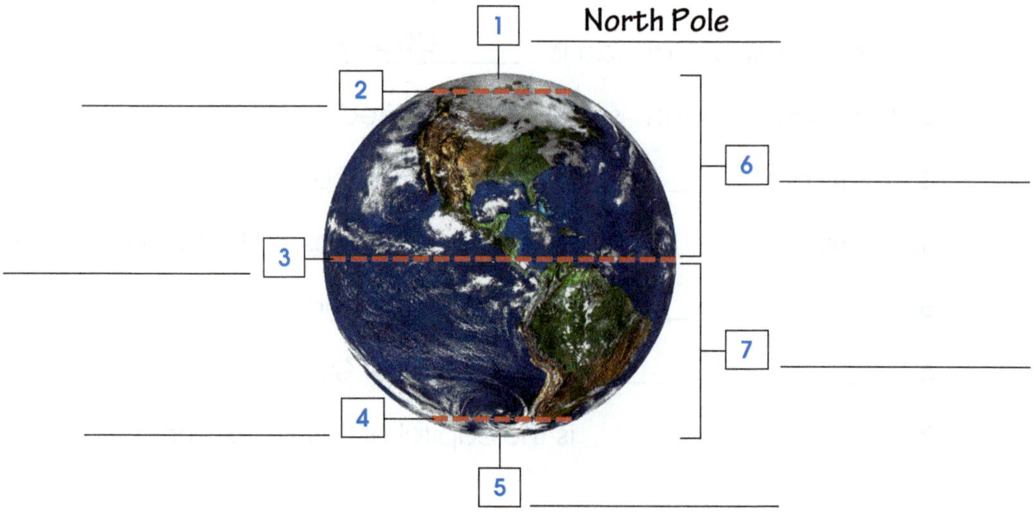

C Write the names of three countries on each continent.

Europe	Asia	Africa	South America
______	______	______	______
______	______	______	______
______	______	______	______

Grammar Connection: Present Perfect Tense

I have visited	Brazil.
I have never visited	Russia.

D Complete the sentences about yourself. Use the names of states or countries.

1. I have visited ______________________________.
2. I have visited ______________________________.
3. I have never visited ______________________________.
4. I have never visited ______________________________.

CD 2
Track 29

E Listen. Write the names of the correct countries.

Pakistan	Brazil	~~China~~
India	Indonesia	Nigeria
Bangladesh	United States	

1. ____China____ 1,350,000,000
2. ______________ 1,250,000,000
3. ______________ 315,000,000
4. ______________ 243,000,000
5. ______________ 199,000,000
6. ______________ 190,000,000
7. ______________ 165,000,000
8. ______________ 159,000,000

F Use the information to complete the sentences.

Continent	Population	Size
Asia	4,200,000,000	17,000,000 square miles
Africa	1,100,000,000	12,000,000 square miles
Europe	734,000,000	4,000,000 square miles
North America	544,000,000	9,500,000 square miles
South America	400,000,000	7,000,000 square miles
Australia	23,000,000	3,000,000 square miles
Antarctica	0	5,400,000 square miles

1. ____Asia____ is the largest continent.
2. ______________ is the smallest continent.
3. ______________ has the most people.
4. No one lives in ______________.
5. South America has more people than ______________.
6. There are more than 3,000,000,000 people in ______________.

The Universe

A Write the word for each item or person.

a space shuttle	a telescope	a space station
a satellite	~~an astronaut~~	a rocket

1. an astronaut

2. ______________

3. ______________

4. ______________

5. ______________

6. ______________

B Circle the correct word.

1. The [(sun) astronaut] is a ball of fire.
2. We look at the stars with a [meteor telescope].
3. An [astronomer eclipse] studies space.
4. [Neptune Mars] is the farthest planet from the sun.
5. Earth has one [rocket moon].
6. An [astronaut orbit] is a person who travels into space.
7. There are millions of [stars space stations] in the sky.
8. A [satellite galaxy] is a large group of stars.
9. [Venus Saturn] has rings.
10. A [constellation rocket] is a group of stars that make a picture.

Grammar Connection: Superlative Adjectives

Neptune is **the coldest** planet.
Venus is **the brightest** planet.

C Write the superlative form of each adjective.

1. Mercury is the closest planet to the sun. (close)
2. Jupiter is ______________ planet. (large)
3. Mercury is ______________ planet. (small)
4. Earth is ______________ planet. (green)
5. Venus is ______________ planet. (hot)
6. Neptune is ______________ planet. (cold)

D Listen to each fact about the planets. Write the name of the correct planet.

CD 2
Track 30

1. Jupiter
2. ______________
3. ______________
4. ______________
5. ______________
6. ______________
7. ______________

Earth
Uranus
Venus
Saturn
~~Jupiter~~
Mars
Mercury

Word Study

Choose a few words from each page. Write each word in a sentence. When you write a sentence, you think more carefully about each word. This will help you to remember the word.

It's cloudy and windy today. It's cool.
I live near the Pacific Ocean.
There is some litter on the street.

Garden

A **Write the word for each flower.**

a rose	a sunflower	~~a daisy~~	a marigold
a daffodil	a tulip	an iris	a lily

1. a daisy

2. ______

3. ______

4. ______

5. ______

6. ______

7. ______

8. ______

B **Look at the picture of the garden in your dictionary. Write two kinds of flowers for each color.**

1. white chrysanthemums daisies
2. yellow ______ ______
3. red ______ ______
4. purple ______ ______
5. orange ______ ______

C **Write the missing letters for these trees.**

1. b i r c h
2. wil ___ ___ ___
3. el ___
4. oa ___
5. ma ___ ___ e
6. p ___ n ___

Grammar Connection: *I think it's a. . . .*

I think	it's	a daisy.

Note:

- Use *I think* when you are not sure about something.

D Read the description. Answer the questions with *I think.*

1. What kind of flower is this? It has yellow petals and a brown center.

   I think it's a sunflower.

2. What kind of flower is this? It has purple and yellow petals.

   ____

3. What kind of flower is this? It's short. It was purple petals and a white center.

   ____

4. What kind of flower is this? The petals are light orange and dark orange.

   ____

5. What kind of flower is this? It's very beautiful and it's red.

   ____

CD 2
Track 31

E Listen to each sentence. Circle the flower you hear.

	a.	b.	c.
1.	a. geraniums	b. marigolds (circled)	c. violets
2.	a. roses	b. tulips	c. irises
3.	a. violets	b. lilies	c. poppies
4.	a. lilies	b. irises	c. ivy
5.	a. daffodils	b. daises	c. poppies
6.	a. chrysanthemums	b. geraniums	c. sunflowers
7.	a. roses	b. violets	c. tulips

F Complete the sentences.

1. My favorite flowers are ______________________
2. Two common trees in my area are ______________________ and ______________________.
3. Two common flowers in my area are ______________________ and ______________________.

Desert

A **Write the word for each animal.**

an ant	a camel	a hawk
a grasshopper	a lizard	~~a mountain lion~~
a scorpion	a tortoise	a snake

1. a mountain lion

2. ____________

3. ____________

4. ____________

5. ____________

6. ____________

7. ____________

8. ____________

9. ____________

B **Write each word in the correct group.**

~~hawk~~	coyote	owl
moth	cricket	mountain lion
spider	vulture	camel

Animals	Birds	Insects
	hawk	

Grammar Connection: Comparative Adjectives

A mountain lion is **larger than** a coyote.
A cricket is **noisier than** a spider.
A scorpion is **more dangerous than** a grasshopper.

Note:

- Comparative adjectives compare two or more people, places, or things.
- For one-syllable adjectives, add *er* + *than*.
- For two-syllable adjectives ending in *y*, change the *y* to *i* and add *er* + *than*.
- For other adjectives with two or more syllables, add *more than* before the adjective.

C Complete each sentence with the name of an animal from the desert.

1. A mountain lion is stronger than a ____________________.
2. A coyote is faster than a ____________________.
3. A moth is prettier than a ____________________.
4. A camel is larger than a ____________________.
5. A turtle is slower than a ____________________.
6. A snake is more dangerous than a ____________________.
7. A scorpion is more frightening than a ____________________.

CD 2
Track 32

D Listen to each animal fact. Write the animal you hear.

grasshopper	scorpion	~~tortoise~~	lizard
camel	mountain lion	spiders	rat

1. tortoise
2. ____________________
3. ____________________
4. ____________________
5. ____________________
6. ____________________
7. ____________________
8. ____________________

E Find the words.

S	C	O	R	P	I	O	N
O	W	L	A	N	T	A	C
C	A	C	T	U	S	S	A
R	S	N	A	K	E	I	M
T	O	R	T	O	I	S	E
U	C	O	Y	O	T	E	L

~~scorpion~~	rat	owl
oasis	cactus	tortoise
camel	snake	coyote
ant		

Rain Forest

A Write the word for each animal.

a parrot	~~a hummingbird~~	a frog
an alligator	a butterfly	a tarantula

1. a hummingbird
2. ______
3. ______

4. ______
5. ______
6. ______

B Read the description of each animal in Exercise A. Write the correct number next to the description.

1. Insects have six legs. This animal has eight legs. 2
2. This large animal has a big mouth and big teeth. It likes to lie in the sun and swim in the water. ____
3. This is the smallest bird in the world. ____
4. This small animal can live on the land or in the water. It can jump and swim. It eats insects. ____
5. This colorful bid is very intelligent. You can teach it to say many words. ____
6. This insect has four large wings. Its wings can have beautiful colors. ____

Grammar Connection: Superlative Adjectives

A whale is **the largest** animal.
A monkey is **the noisiest** animal.
A lion is **the most dangerous** animal.

Note:

- Superlative adjectives compare three or more people, places, or things.
- For one-syllable adjectives, add *the* + *est*.
- For two-syllable adjectives ending in *y*, change the *y* to *i* and add *the* + *est*.
- For other adjectives with two or more syllables, add *the most* before the adjective.

C Complete each sentence with the name of an animal from the rain forest.

1. A ______________________ is the slowest animal.
2. A ______________________ is the fastest animal.
3. A ______________________ is the largest animal.
4. A ______________________ is the strongest animal.
5. A ______________________ is the smallest animal.
6. A ______________________ is the most poisonous animal.
7. A ______________________ is the noisiest animal.
8. A ______________________ is the most interesting animal.
9. A ______________________ is the prettiest animal.

CD 2
Track 33

D Where do these animals live? Listen and match the animal and the country or continent.

<u>c</u>	1. aardvarks	a. Every country
____	2. alligators	b. India and Sri Lanka
____	3. crocodiles	c. Africa
____	4. frogs	d. Sumatra and Borneo
____	5. orangutans	e. Florida and China
____	6. panthers	f. Australia and Southeast Asia
____	7. peacocks	g. North and South America
____	8. tigers	h. India, China, Indonesia, Siberia

E Write the names of four animals that live in your country.

______________________ ______________________

______________________ ______________________

Grasslands

A **Read the information in the chart. Then complete the sentences about each animal.**

How long does each animal live?

antelope	10–25 years	leopard	12–15 years
buffalo	18–25 years	lion	15 years
elephant	50–70 years	rhinoceros	40–45 years
giraffe	15–20 years	zebra	25 years
hippopotamus	45 years		

1. A rhinoceros lives 40–45 years.

2. A ________ lives ________ years.

3. A ________ lives ________ years.

4. A ________ lives ________ years.

5. An ________ lives ________ years.

6. A ________ lives ________ years.

7. A ________ lives ________ years.

8. A ________ lives ________ years.

9. An ________ lives ________ years.

Grammar Connection: *Has*

A giraffe	**has**	a long tail.
A zebra	**has**	hooves.

B **Write a sentence about an animal that has each feature.**

1. a short tail: A hippopotamus has a short tail.
2. a trunk: ____________________
3. horns: ____________________
4. tusks: ____________________
5. antlers: ____________________
6. hooves: ____________________
7. a mane: ____________________
8. paws: ____________________
9. fur: ____________________

C **Look at the picture of the grasslands. Circle *T* if the statement is true. Circle *F* is the statement is false.**

1. A zebra is larger than a rhinoceros. T F
2. A cheetah is faster than a hippopotamus. T F
3. A lion is more dangerous than a gazelle. T F
4. A hyena is smaller than a leopard. T F
5. An antelope is stronger than an elephant. T F

CD 2
Track 34

D **Listen to two children talk about their trip to the zoo. Write the number of each statement under the correct animal.**

hyenas	elephants	kangaroos	ostriches
____	____	1	____
cheetahs	lions	koalas	giraffes
____	____	____	____

Polar Lands

A **Write the word for each polar animal.**

a seal	a penguin	a grizzly bear
a whale	~~a wolf~~	a moose

1. a wolf
2. ______
3. ______

4. ______
5. ______
6. ______

B **Look at the picture of the polar lands in your dictionary. Circle *T* if the statement is true. Circle *F* if the statement is false.**

1. A polar bear has tusks. T (F)
2. A grizzly bear is white. T F
3. A seal has flippers. T F
4. A falcon has claws. T F
5. A fox is larger than a wolf. T F
6. A goose has a beak. T F
7. An otter has brown fur. T F
8. A baby bear is a cub. T F

Grammar Connection: *Which* Questions and Answers

Which animal	has	flippers and a long beak?		**A penguin does.**

C Answer the questions about animals of the polar lands.

1. Which animal has flippers, white fur, and a black tail? A seal does.
2. Which animal has brown fur and large antlers? ______________
3. Which animal has a short beak and strong claws? ______________
4. Which large animal has white fur? ______________
5. Which animal has flippers and two long tusks? ______________
6. Which animal flies south in the winter? ______________
7. Which animal lives in the water but comes up for air? ______________

CD 2
Track 35

D Listen to each animal fact. Write the number of the statement under the correct picture.

a. ______________

b. ______________

c. 1

d. ______________

e. ______________

f. ______________

g. ______________

h. ______________

E Look at the picture of the polar lands in your dictionary. Find one or more animals with each feature.

1. tusks: walrus.
2. feathers: ______________
3. wings: ______________
4. flippers: ______________
5. a beak: ______________
6. whiskers: ______________

Sea

A **Write the word for each sea animal.**

a shark	a sea horse	an angelfish	a turtle
a starfish	a squid	a stingray	~~a sea anemone~~

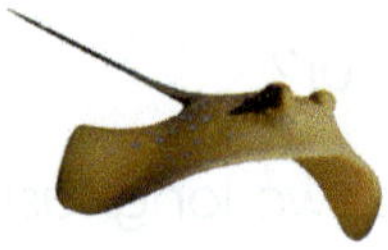

1. a sea anemone
2. ______
3. ______
4. ______

5. ______
6. ______
7. ______
8. ______

B **Draw four fish in this aquarium. Write the name of each fish.**

Grammar Connection: Simple Present Tense - *Yes/No* Questions

Does	a turtle	**have**	a hard shell?
Do	turtles	**have**	hard shells?

Yes,	it **does**.
Yes,	they **do**.

Note:

- For simple present tense questions, use *does* for third person singular.
- For simple present tense questions, use *do* for third person plural.

C Complete the questions with *do* or *does*. Then, write the short answer.

1. ________ sharks have sharp teeth? Yes, they do.
2. ________ a shark eat other fish? Yes, it does.
3. ________ a sea horse move slowly? Yes, ________
4. ________ sea horses like warm water? Yes, ________
5. ________ crabs have two claws? Yes, ________
6. ________ an eel look like a snake? Yes, ________
7. ________ a halibut lie at the bottom of the sea? Yes, ________
8. ________ a starfish have five arms? Yes, ________
9. ________ dolphins breathe air? Yes, ________
10. ________ stingrays live on the ocean floor? Yes, ________
11. ________ a tuna have fins? Yes, ________
12. ________ orcas hunt large fish? Yes, ________

CD 2
Track 36

D Listen to the information about the length of these sea animals. Complete the chart below.

1. stingray	7 feet
2. ________	8 feet
3. giant ________	15 feet
4. ________	16 feet
5. ________	23 feet
6. killer ________	30 feet
7. giant ________	60 feet

squid
dolphin
~~stingray~~
octopus
whale
shark
swordfish

Woodlands

A Complete the crossword puzzle.

Across

2 

4 

5 

9 

10 

11 

Down

1 

6 

8 

3 

7 

B Write the words in the correct group.

hornet	tick	squirrel	porcupine	duck
robin	~~chipmunk~~	dragonfly	eagle	blue jay
woodpecker	rabbit	ladybug	groundhog	mosquito

Animals	Birds	Insects
chipmunk		

Grammar Connection: Simple Present Tense - Third Person Statements

Robins Eagles	**sing** **build**	all day. large nests.

A robin An eagle	**sings** **builds**	all day. a large nest.

Note:

- For the simple present tense, add an *s* to the third person singular verb.

C Change these sentences from the plural to the singular.

1. Moles live underground — A mole lives underground.
2. Cardinals eat worms. ______________
3. Squirrels look for nuts. ______________
4. Dragonflies have four wings. ______________
5. Wasps sting. ______________
6. Bobcats move quietly. ______________
7. Skunks smell terrible. ______________

CD 2
Track 37

D Listen to each speaker. Circle the animal you hear.

1.	**a.** mosquito	**b.** eagle (circled)	**c.** beaver
2.	**a.** toad	**b.** raccoon	**c.** robin
3.	**a.** blue jay	**b.** bobcat	**c.** robin
4.	**a.** skunk	**b.** squirrel	**c.** mouse
5.	**a.** duck	**b.** nest	**c.** deer
6.	**a.** dragonfly	**b.** woodpecker	**c.** salamander
7.	**a.** turkey	**b.** toad	**c.** eagle

Word Study

It helps to group words in different ways. In this unit, you learned the names of many animals. You can group these words many ways: large animals and small animals; animals with two legs, four legs, six legs, and eight legs; animals I see near my home; etc.

Math

A **Write the word for the shape or solid that makes up each item.**

a square	a cone	a circle	~~an oval~~
a sphere	a rectangle	a triangle	a cube

1. *an oval*

2. ______

3. ______

4. ______

5. ______

6. ______

7. ______

8. ______

B **Draw the lines.**

1. a straight line
2. a curved line
3. parallel lines
4. perpendicular lines

C **Match.**

c	1. plus	a.	−
____	2. minus	b.	½
____	3. equals	c.	+
____	4. percent	d.	÷
____	5. multiplied by	e.	=
____	6. divided by	f.	%
____	7. a fraction	g.	×

Grammar Connection: Math Problems

Five **plus** ten is fifteen.
Twenty **minus** ten is ten.
Five **times** four is twenty.
Five **multiplied by** four is twenty.
Six **divided by** two is three.

D **Solve the problem. Write the problem as a sentence.**

a. 2 + 8 Two plus eight is ten.

b. 12 − 5 ____________

c. 3 × 5 ____________

d. 7 + 4 ____________

e. 10 ÷ 2 ____________

f. 3 × 4 ____________

g. 20 − 10 ____________

E **Look in your dictionary. Can you draw the shapes and solids?**

1. rectangle **2.** oval **3.** triangle **4.** cube **5.** cylinder

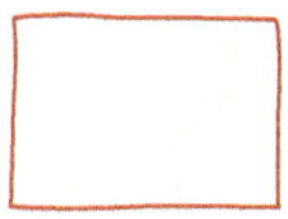

CD 2
Track 38

F **Listen and complete each math problem. Then solve the problem.**

a. 10 __+__ 5 = __15__

b. 3 ____ 3 = ____

c. 8 ____ 5 = ____

d. 10 ____ 5 = ____

e. 6 ____ 7 = ____

f. 12 ____ 5 = ____

g. 8 ____ 2 = ____

h. 10 ____ 5 = ____

i. 20 ____ 5 = ____

j. 10 ____ 5 ____ 2 = ____

Science

A Complete the crossword puzzle.

Across

1 

5 

9 

10 

11 

12 

13 

Down

2 

3 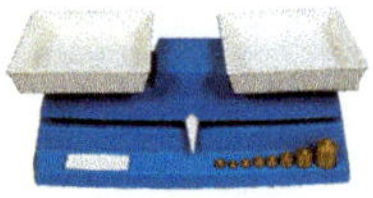

4 

6 

7 

8 

B Cross out the word that does not belong.

1. beaker	flask	~~gas~~	graduated cylinder
2. biology	stopper	chemistry	physics
3. forceps	element	atom	molecule
4. funnel	physicist	chemist	biologist
5. solid	liquid	gas	magnet

Grammar Connection: Affirmative and Negative Instructions

Light the Bunsen burner. **Measure** the liquid.	**Don't light** the Bunsen burner. **Don't measure** the liquid.

C Write the negative of each instruction.

1. Place the sample on the slide. Don't place the sample on the slide.
2. Turn off the Bunsen burner. ____________________
3. Boil the liquid. ____________________
4. Pick up the solid. ____________________
5. Pour liquid into the flask. ____________________
6. Use the magnifying glass. ____________________
7. Fill the beaker with water. ____________________

D Listen to these science lab instructions. Complete the sentences.

CD 2
Track 39

1. Light the Bunsen burner.
2. Clean the ____________________.
3. Cover the ____________________.
4. Hold the ____________________ in the sunlight.
5. Hand me the ____________________.
6. Count the ____________________ you see.
7. Remove some liquid with the ____________________.
8. Fill the ____________________ with the blue liquid.

atoms
petri dish
~~Bunsen burner~~
forceps
test tube
dropper
slide
prism

E Complete with information about yourself.

1. I studied biology. Yes No
2. I studied chemistry. Yes No
3. I studied physics. Yes No
4. Another science I studied is ____________________.

Writing

A **Write the word for each punctuation mark.**

a period	a question mark	quotation marks	~~an apostrophe~~
a comma	an exclamation point	parentheses	a hyphen

1. ' an apostrophe
2. ? ____________
3. - ____________
4. , ____________
5. ! ____________
6. " " ____________
7. ( ) ____________
8. . ____________

B **Add the punctuation in the yellow space.**

1. Add a period: Open your dictionary .
2. Add quotation marks: The teacher said, __ Open your dictionary. __
3. Add a question mark: Do you have your dictionary today __
4. Add a comma: I have my dictionary __ but I forgot my workbook.
5. Add an apostrophe: My dictionary isn __ t in my backpack.
6. Add a hyphen: *Book* is a one __ syllable word.
7. Add a colon: Please bring the following items to class tomorrow __ your dictionary, your workbook, and a notebook.
8. Add parentheses: The word *dictionary* has four syllables __ dic·tion·ar·y __ .
9. Add an exclamation point: Wonderful __

C **Put the steps in order.**

____ Write an outline.

____ Type your final draft.

____ Write a draft.

____ Get feedback.

__1__ Brainstorm.

____ Edit your essay.

Grammar Connection: *Before* and *After*

After you write an outline, write a draft.
Before you write a draft, write an outline.

D Begin each sentence with *Before* or *After*.

1. Before you write, brainstorm ideas.
2. ________ you write a draft, get feedback from another student.
3. ________ you type your final draft, edit your essay.
4. ________ you type your final draft, check the punctuation.
5. ________ you type your final draft, give your paper to the teacher.

E Look at the writing. Circle *T* if the statement is true. Circle *F* if the statement is false.

Vocabulary Notebooks

Several students in my class say that a vocabulary notebook helps them to study and remember vocabulary. Each student has a different system. One student writes a word in English. Then, he writes the word in his native language. Another student draws a picture. Then, she writes the word next to it. In my vocabulary notebook, I write the new word. Then, I write it in a sentence. We all carry our notebooks with us and review the words for a few minutes each day.

1. This is an essay.	T	(F)
2. This is a paragraph.	T	F
3. There are eleven sentences in this paragraph.	T	F
4. The title of this paragraph is *Vocabulary Study.*	T	F
5. There is a margin on the left.	T	F

CD 2
Track 40

F Listen and write the punctuation mark you hear.

1. ! **3.** ____ **5.** ____ **7.** ____

2. ____ **4.** ____ **6.** ____ **8.** ____

Explore, Rule, Invent

A **Write the word for each picture.**

built	sailed	~~grew~~
flew	launched	won

1. grew

2. ______

3. ______

4. ______

5. ______

6. ______

B **Circle the correct word.**

1. The musician [(composed) won] music.
2. The scientist [discovered flew] a cure for the disease.
3. The soldiers [introduced defended] their country.
4. The people [migrated elected] a new president.
5. The king [grew ruled] the country for many years.
6. The company [introduced fell] a new product.
7. The workers [discovered built] a bridge.
8. The woman [won sailed] the Nobel Peace Prize.
9. The farmers [invented grew] vegetables and fruit.

Grammar Connection: Simple Past Tense - Statements

I **explored** the island.
He **sailed** around the world.
They **won** the prize.

Note:

- Regular past tense verbs end in *d* or *ed*.
- Many verbs are irregular in the past tense:
  build - built fall - fell fly - flew grow - grew win - won
- The past tense is the same for all persons, singular and plural.

C Complete the sentences with the correct past tense verb.

discovered
composed
introduced
ended
built
~~invented~~
opened

1. Alexander Graham Bell ___invented___ the telephone.
2. Workers ______________ the Empire State Building.
3. Sir Alexander Fleming ______________ penicillin.
4. The Panama Canal ______________ in 1914.
5. Mozart ______________ many symphonies.
6. Apple Computer ______________ the iPhone in 2007.
7. World War II ______________ in 1945.

CD 2
Track 41

D Listen and complete the sentences.

won	produced	~~invented~~	flew	built
introduced	discovered	reached	ended	opened

1. 1850 Elisha Otis ___invented___ the modern elevator.
2. 1927 Charles Lindbergh ______________ across the Atlantic.
3. 1937 The Golden Gate Bridge ______________ over San Francisco Bay.
4. 1953 Hillary and Norgay ______________ the top of Mount Everest.
5. 1955 Jonas Salk ______________ the polio vaccine.
6. 1975 The Vietnam War ______________.
7. 1979 Mother Teresa ______________ the Nobel Peace Prize.
8. 1981 IBM ______________ the first personal computer.
9. 1986-94 Workers ______________ a tunnel between England and France.
10. 1994 Kodak ______________ the first digital camera for consumers.

U.S. Government and Citizenship

A **Write the building for each branch of the U.S. government.**

the Supreme Court	the Capitol Building	the White House

Executive branch:

1. ______________________________

Legislative branch:

2. ______________________________

Judicial branch:

3. ______________________________

B **Write each person under the correct branch of government.**

senator	~~president~~	justice
vice president	congressman	congresswoman

Executive	**Legislative**	**Judicial**
president	____________	____________
____________	____________	
	____________	

Grammar Connection: *Wh-* Question Words

Who – person	*How many* – number
When – time	*How long* – length of time
Where – place	*How old* – age

C Circle the correct question word. Try to answer the questions.

1. [Who When] is the President of the United States? ____________________
2. [When How many] is the election? ____________________
3. [How long How many] is one term as President? ____________________
4. [When Where] does the President live? ____________________
5. [When Who] becomes President if the president dies? ____________________
6. [How many How old] must the President be? ____________________
7. [How long How many] is the President's term in office? ____________________
8. [Who Why] can vote? ____________________

CD 2
Track 42

D Listen and circle the correct branch of government for each person or place.

1. legislative executive judicial
2. legislative executive judicial
3. legislative executive judicial
4. legislative executive judicial
5. legislative executive judicial
6. legislative executive judicial
7. legislative executive judicial
8. legislative executive judicial

E Complete the information.

1. ____________________ is the president of the United States.
2. ____________________ is the vice president of the United States.
3. There [is isn't] a president in my country.
4. The leader of my country is ____________________.

Word Study

Some English words may sound similar to words in your own language. For example, maybe a word starts with the same sound in both English and your first language. Noticing these similarities can help you remember the English word.

Fine Arts

A **Write the words for the kind of art and for the artist.**

pottery	a photograph	a sculpture	~~a painting~~
a photographer	~~a painter~~	a potter	a sculptor

1. a painting
2. a painter
3. ______
4. ______
5. ______
6. ______
7. ______
8. ______

B **Complete the sentences.**

paint	~~painter~~	paintbrush	palette	canvas

1. The painter is painting a picture.
2. There is a ______ on the easel.
3. She is holding a ______ in her right hand.
4. There is a ______ in her left hand.
5. The ______ is on the table.

C **Cross out the word that does not belong.**

1. still life	~~sculptor~~	portrait	landscape
2. easel	canvas	clay	sketch pad
3. palette	pottery	clay	potter's wheel
4. sketch	potter	photographer	sculptor
5. palette	paint	paintbrush	pottery

Grammar Connection: Professions with *-er* and *-or*

teach**er**	photograph**er**	doct**or**	janit**or**
paint**er**	pott**er**	sculpt**or**	act**or**

Note:

- Many jobs and professions end in *-er* or *-or*.

D Circle the correct word in each sentence.

1. The [painter   painting] is in a frame.
2. Picasso is a famous [painter   painting].
3. He took a [photographer   photograph] of his children.
4. The [photographer   photograph] is taking pictures of the model.
5. There is a large [sculptor   sculpture] outside the museum.
6. A [sculptor   sculpture] uses marble, stone, wood or other materials.
7. The [potter   pottery] made a beautiful flower vase.
8. The [potter   pottery] has to dry before she can paint it.

CD 2
Track 43

E Listen to each statement. Write the number of the statement under the correct picture.

a. ______

b. ______

c. ___1___

d. ______

e. ______

f. ______

Performing Arts

A **Look at the picture of the opera. Circle *T* if the statement is true. Circle *F* if the statement is false.**

1. The woman is an opera singer.	(T)	F
2. She is on a stage.	T	F
3. She is holding a microphone.	T	F
4. She is bowing.	T	F
5. There are spotlights on her.	T	F
6. She is wearing a costume.	T	F
7. She is wearing a mask.	T	F
8. There is an orchestra.	T	F

B **Find the words.**

(G U I T A R I S T)
B A L C O N Y I I
A C M A S K O N C
L T U S E A T G K
L O S S T A G E E
E R C O N C E R T
T I P R O G R A M

actor	ballet
~~guitarist~~	balcony
ticket	singer
concert	stage
program	seat
mask	set

Grammar Connection: Simple Past Tense – *Wh-* Questions

Where What What group	did	you	go? do? see?

C Write the correct question for each answer

Where did you sit?
What group did you see?
~~What did you do last weekend?~~
How did you like the show?
Who did you go with?

1. What did you do last weekend?
   I went to a rock concert.
2. ______________________
   I saw Rock Out.
3. ______________________
   I went with my cousins.
4. ______________________
   We sat near the stage.
5. ______________________
   It was great!

CD 2
Track 44

D Listen to each speaker. Check the kind(s) of performance(s) each speaker enjoys.

	Ballet	Rock Concerts	Plays	Opera
1.	✓	____	____	____
2.	____	____	____	____
3.	____	____	____	____
4.	____	____	____	____

E Circle the correct word.

1. People buy tickets at the [costume **box office**].
2. The [usher singer] shows people to their seats.
3. The usher gives each person a [spotlight program].
4. People can sit in the [balcony mask].
5. The theater is full. There are no more [stages seats].
6. The [audience mask] watches a play.
7. An [usher orchestra] plays music.
8. Actors can wear [costumes conductors].
9. Singers sometimes hold a [set microphone].
10. After the ballet, the dancers [bow clap]. The audience [bows claps].

Instruments

A Write the word for each instrument.

a harmonica	drums	a trumpet	a guitar
a piano	~~a sitar~~	a French horn	a saxophone
a harp	maracas	pan pipes	a tambourine

1. a sitar

2. ____________

3. ____________

4. ____________

5. ____________

6. ____________

7. ____________

8. ____________

9. ____________

10. ____________

11. ____________

12. ____________

B Cross out the word that does not belong.

1. bass	cello	banjo	~~electric keyboard~~
2. drums	maracas	bugle	cymbals
3. oboe	clarinet	saxophone	harp
4. accordion	trombone	organ	piano
5. tambourine	trumpet	French horn	tuba
6. guitar	bassoon	violin	sitar

Grammar Connection: *How well...?*

How well do you play the piano?	I can't play the piano. I'm just beginning. I'm not very good. I'm pretty good. I'm in a band. I'm a professional.

Note:

- Use *How well* to ask people about their skill level with something.

C Answer each question. Use different answers from the grammar chart.

1. How well do you play the piano? I'm pretty good.
2. How well do you play the trumpet? ______
3. How well do you play the drums? ______
4. How well do you play the guitar? ______
5. How well do you play the maracas? ______
6. How well do you play the harmonica? ______

CD 2 Track 45

D Listen and circle the instrument you hear.

1. **a.** trumpet **(b.)** guitar **c.** cymbals
2. **a.** piano **b.** clarinet **c.** violin
3. **a.** maracas **b.** saxophone **c.** organ
4. **a.** banjo **b.** tuba **c.** harp
5. **a.** accordion **b.** piano **c.** bass
6. **a.** violin **b.** tuba **c.** marimba
7. **a.** sitar **b.** pan pipes **c.** trumpet
8. **a.** bass **b.** trombone **c.** harmonica
9. **a.** oboe **b.** guitar **c.** drums
10. **a.** cello **b.** tambourine **c.** flute

E Complete with information about yourself.

1. I would like to play the ______.
2. The ______ is a popular instrument in my country.
3. My favorite instrument is the ______.

Film, TV, and Music

A Each picture is from a movie or TV show. Write the word for each kind of movie or TV show.

romance	sports	action
western	~~nature program~~	horror

1. nature program
2. ______
3. ______

4. ______
5. ______
6. ______

B Write each word in the correct group.

~~action~~	horror	jazz	western
news	reality show	soap opera	rock
hip hop	comedy	classical	sports

Films / Movies	TV Programs	Music
action		

Grammar Connection: *What kind of…?*

What kind of	music	do you enjoy? do you like? do you listen to?

I enjoy **country** music.
I like **classical** music.
I listen to **rock** music.

Note:

- *What kind of asks* for specific information.

C Answer the questions about yourself.

1. What kind of music do you like?

____

2. What kind of TV programs do you watch?

____

3. What kind of movies do you enjoy?

____

CD 2
Track 46

D Listen and circle the kind of music you hear.

1. a. rock	**b.** jazz	**(c.)** pop
2. a. rock	**b.** classical	**c.** hip hop
3. a. classical	**b.** country and western	**c.** hip hop
4. a. country and western	**b.** rock	**c.** soul
5. a. classical	**b.** hip hop	**c.** blues
6. a. hip hop	**b.** jazz	**c.** country and western
7. a. classical	**b.** country and western	**c.** jazz

Word Study

Be patient with yourself. It takes time to learn new words in English. When you continue to practice and review, your vocabulary will grow little by little, day by day.

Beach

A **Write the word for each beach item.**

a beach ball	water wings	a mask	a pail
a cooler	sunscreen	~~a life jacket~~	fins

1. a life jacket

2. ______

3. ______

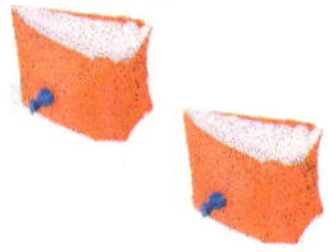

4. ______

5. ______

6. ______

7. ______

8. ______

B **Complete each sentence with a word from Exercise A.**

1. The man is swimming fast. He is wearing ____fins____ on his feet.
2. The children are putting shells in the ______________.
3. My little girl always wears ______________ in the water to help her float.
4. The children are playing with a big ______________.
5. The sodas and sandwiches are in the ______________.
6. The snorkeler is wearing a ______________ on his face.
7. The water-skier is wearing a ______________.
8. It's very sunny. Put on some ______________.

C **Write the missing letters for these beach words.**

1. sunba _t_ _h_ er
2. suns ___ ___ een
3. sailb ___ a ___
4. moto ___ ___ oa ___
5. life ___ uar ___
6. ligh___ ___ ouse

Grammar Connection: Adverbs of Frequency

I **always** wear a belt.
I **often** wear a belt.
I **sometimes** wear a belt.
I **never** wear a belt.

always	90% to 100%
often	70% to 90%
sometimes	30% to 70%
never	0%

Note:

- Put the adverb of frequency before a regular verb.
- Put the adverb of frequency after the verb *be*.
- *Sometimes* can also be used at the beginning or the end of a sentence.

D Put the words in these sentences in order.

1. I always put on sunscreen.
   sunscreen / put on / I / always
2. ____________________
   often / to the beach / we / in the summer / go
3. ____________________
   under / always / we / sit / an umbrella
4. ____________________
   shells / the children / sometimes / collect
5. ____________________
   wear / always / life jackets / my children

CD 2
Track 47

E Look at the picture of the beach in your dictionary. Listen to each question and circle the correct answer.

1. (a.) It's next to the pail. — b. It's on the pier.
2. a. He's wearing a life jacket. — b. He's wearing a snorkel.
3. a. The sunbather is. — b. The lifeguard is.
4. a. There is one. — b. There are seven.
5. a. They are in the sand castle. — b. They are in the cooler.
6. a. It's next to the cooler. — b. It's next to the fins.
7. a. He's wearing a mask. — b. He's wearing water wings.
8. a. It's red. — b. It's white.
9. a. It's in the pail. — b. It's on the sand.
10. a. No one is. — b. The lifeguard is.

Camping

A Complete the sentences.

water bottle	insect repellent	binoculars	backpack	tent
matches	camping stove	~~fishing pole~~	canteen	compass

1. You can fish with a ___fishing pole___.
2. You can carry things in a ____________.
3. You can find your direction with a ____________.
4. You can cook on a ____________.
5. You can carry water in a ____________ or a ____________.
6. You can see far away things with ____________.
7. You can light a fire with ____________.
8. You can sleep in a ____________.
9. You can put on ____________ to keep insects away.

B Look at the picture in your dictionary. Circle *T* if the statement is true. Circle *F* if the statement is false.

1. Someone is in the rowboat. (T) F
2. Someone is in the raft. T F
3. Someone is in the tent. T F
4. Someone is hiking on the trail. T F
5. Someone is cooking on the camping stove. T F
6. Someone is carrying a backpack. T F
7. Someone is using binoculars. T F
8. Someone is enjoying the campfire. T F
9. Someone is in the canoe. T F
10. Someone is in the sleeping bag. T F

Grammar Connection: *Because*

We need sleeping bags **because** it's going to be cold at night.

Note:

- Use *because* to give a reason.

C Complete the sentences with *because* and the reason.

we are going to build a fire	we are going to catch fish
we are going to cook the fish	it's going to be dark at night
~~we are going to hike~~	

1. We need a compass *because we are going to hike.*
2. We need a lantern ______________________
3. We need fishing poles ______________________
4. We need a camping stove ______________________
5. We need matches ______________________

CD 2
Track 48

D Listen to the campers prepare for a camping trip. Write the number of the conversation under the correct item.

a. ____________

b. ____________

c. ____________

d. ____________

e. ____________

f. ____________

g. ____1____

h. ____________

E Circle the outdoor equipment that you have.

a compass	a canteen	a tent
a fishing pole	binoculars	a sleeping bag
a backpack	a pocket knife	____________

City Park

A **Complete the sentences about each picture.**

joggers	cyclist	skateboard	skater
bicycle	~~skateboarder~~	skates	

1. She's a ___skateboarder___.
2. She's on her ______________.
3. He's a ______________.
4. He's riding a ______________.

5. They are ______________.
6. He's a ______________.
7. He's wearing ______________.

B **Circle the correct word.**

1. The horses on the [bridge (carousel)] go around and around.
2. Children climb on the [sandbox jungle gym].
3. The [seesaw bench] goes up and down.
4. There are some ducks in the [pond path].
5. The children are watching a [bench puppet show].
6. People can buy hot dogs from the [roller coaster street vendor].
7. A boy is flying his [kite skates].
8. Put your garbage in the [sandbox trash can].
9. A family is having a [picnic pond] in the park.

Grammar Connection: Past Time Expressions

Last	Ago	Yesterday
last week **last** month **last** year	two days **ago** three weeks **ago** four months **ago**	**yesterday** the day before **yesterday**

Note:

- We usually put a time expression at the end of the sentence.
- We sometimes put a time expression at the beginning of a sentence.

C Rewrite each sentence. Add a time expression.

1. I rode a bicycle. *I rode a bicycle last summer.*
2. The boy flew a kite. ______________________
3. The family had a picnic. ______________________
4. We rode the carousel. ______________________
5. I went to the park. ______________________
6. She fed the pigeons. ______________________
7. They jogged in the park. ______________________
8. He skated in the park. ______________________

CD 2 Track 49

D Listen to a mother describe the park in her area. Check the things in the park.

- ☑ a playground
- ☐ swings
- ☐ monkey bars
- ☐ slides
- ☐ a jungle gym
- ☐ a seesaw
- ☐ a sandbox
- ☐ a roller coaster
- ☐ a carousel
- ☐ a pond
- ☐ picnic tables
- ☐ a path

E Write the name of a park in your area. Circle the things in the park.

______________________ is a park in my area. It has . . . .

a playground	a sandbox	park benches
swings	picnic tables	a pond
a slide	a carousel	a bridge
a jungle gym	a Ferris wheel	paths

Places to Visit

A Write the location or activity.

circus	pool hall	bicycle path
bowling alley	café	sporting event
gym	hiking trail	~~miniature golf~~

1. miniature golf
2. ____________
3. ____________

4. ____________
5. ____________
6. ____________

7. ____________
8. ____________
9. ____________

B Match.

b	1. bowling	a. theater
____	2. botanical	b. alley
____	3. movie	c. sale
____	4. amusement	d. golf
____	5. miniature	e. arcade
____	6. video	f. garden
____	7. garage	g. park

Grammar Connection: *Let's*

Let's go to the amusement park. I love to ride the roller coaster.
Let's go to the nursery. I need some new flowers for the yard.

Note:

- Use *let's* to make a suggestion.
- Use the base form of the verb after *let's*.

C Make a suggestion. Begin each sentence with *Let's go to the.*

1. Let's go to the zoo. They have a new panda.
2. ________________ The kids like to watch the dolphins.
3. ________________ The roses are all in bloom.
4. ________________ There's a new adventure film playing.
5. ________________ It's so hot and the kids love the water.
6. ________________ I love to watch the horses.
7. ________________ We might find some good bargains.
8. ________________ I need to exercise.

CD 2
Track 50

D Listen to each speaker. Where is each person?

1. carnival
2. ________________
3. ________________
4. ________________
5. ________________
6. ________________
7. ________________

sporting event
café
~~carnival~~
garage sale
botanical garden
zoo
planetarium

E Look at the places in your dictionary. Where do you go . . .

1. on a rainy day? ________________
2. on a warm, sunny day? ________________
3. when your friends come to visit? ________________
4. on a Saturday evening? ________________
5. with young children? ________________

Indoor Sports and Fitness

A Match the picture and the action.

a

b

c

d

e

f

g

h

1. The weightlifter can lift 150 pounds. g
2. This person can do 50 sit-ups. ____
3. This person uses the stationary bicycle four times a week. ____
4. This person does yoga in the evenings. ____
5. This person teaches martial arts. ____
6. This person does 25 push-ups every morning. ____
7. This person plays basketball after work. ____
8. This boxer trains five days a week. ____

B Circle the athletes.

darts	a boxer	a bench	a gymnast
a wrestler	a barbell	a referee	a treadmill
a basketball player	a fitness class	a diver	a weightlifter

Grammar Connection: Modal - *can*

My brother	**can lift**	weights.
My mother	**can swim**	in the pool.

Note:

- Use *can* to show that something is possible.
- Use the base form of the verb after *can*.

C Your family just joined a gym. Using the word box, write activities each of your family members can enjoy.

take a yoga class	play volleyball	ride a stationary bicycle
~~walk on a treadmill~~	play ping-pong	join the boxing team
take a fitness class	swim in the pool	

1. My father can walk on a treadmill.
2. ______
3. ______
4. ______
5. ______
6. ______

CD 2
Track 51

D Listen to each speaker. What sport or activity does each person enjoy at the gym?

1. stationary bike
2. ______
3. ______
4. ______
5. ______
6. ______
7. ______

yoga
weightlifting
treadmill
~~stationary bike~~
ping-pong
martial arts
fitness class

Outdoor Sports and Fitness

A In which sport do you use each ball?

golf	football	soccer
baseball	volleyball	~~tennis~~

1. tennis
2. __________
3. __________

4. __________
5. __________
6. __________

B Write the person.

1. A batter hits a baseball.
2. A __________ catches a baseball.
3. A __________ hits a golf ball.
4. A __________ watches a sports game.
5. A __________ runs on a track.
6. A __________ does cheers for the players.

catcher
cheerleader
fan
golfer
~~batter~~
runner

C Write the sport(s) next to the equipment.

1. bat: __________
2. club: __________
3. helmet: __________

4. racket: ________________

5. net: ________________ ________________

6. goalpost: ________________ ________________

Grammar Connection: *There are* with *some* and *any*

There are some baseball fields in our town.
There aren't any baseball fields in our town.

Note:

- Use *There are some* before a noun in an affirmative statement.
- Use *There aren't any* before the noun in a negative statement.

D **Complete the sentences about the town or city where you live now. Use *There are some* or *There aren't any*.**

1. ___There are some___ baseball fields in this city.
2. ________________ tennis courts in this city.
3. ________________ soccer fields in this city.
4. ________________ golf courses in this city.
5. ________________ football fields in this city.
6. ________________ track fields in this city.
7. ________________ volleyball courts in this city.

CD 2
Track 52

E **Listen to the sports reporter. Write the name of the correct sport.**

1. ___volleyball___
2. ________________
3. ________________
4. ________________
5. ________________
6. ________________

football
golf
~~volleyball~~
tennis
baseball
soccer

Winter Sports

A Look at the picture in your dictionary. How many do you see?

1. ice skaters 2
2. hockey players ____
3. skiers ____
4. snowboarders ____
5. skis ____
6. snowmobiles ____
7. toboggans ____
8. sleds ____
9. chairs on the chairlift ____
10. hockey sticks ____

B Cross out the word that does not belong.

1. snowmobile	~~goal~~	toboggan	sled
2. skis	ski boots	ski poles	snowshoes
3. sled	rink	puck	hockey stick
4. ice skates	ice skater	chairlift	ice skating
5. goal	snowshoes	ski boots	ice skates
6. skier	snowboarder	ice skater	hockey stick

Grammar Connection: *good / better / best*

I am a **good** ice skater.
Tony is a **better** ice skater than **me**.
Sam is **the best** ice skater on the team.

C Complete the sentences with the correct form of the adjective.

1. I am a good skier.
2. Melissa is a better skier than me.
3. Emma is the best skier on the team.

4. I am a ________ hockey player.

5. Jason is a ________ hockey player ________ me.

6. Ken is the ________ hockey player on the team.

7. I am a ________ snowboarder.

8. Martin is a ________ snowboarder ________ me.

9. Brian is ________ snowboarder on the team.

CD 2
Track 53

D Listen and write the number of each conversation under the correct picture.

a. ________

b. ________

c. 1

d. ________

e. ________

f. ________

E Complete with information about yourself.

1. We [have do not have] winter in my country.
2. It [never sometimes often] snows in my country.
3. I enjoy [skiing snowboarding ice skating ice hockey].
4. I have never tried [skiing snowboarding ice skating ice hockey].

Games, Toys, and Hobbies

A Write the word for each game.

dice	chess	backgammon
checkers	~~dominoes~~	mah-jongg

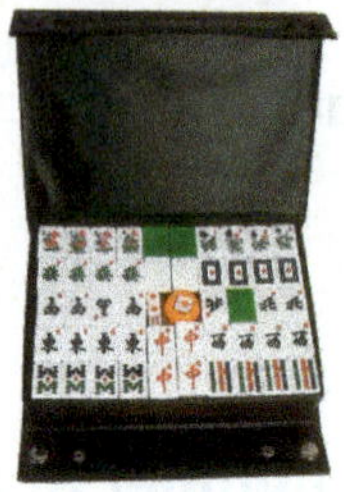

1. dominoes
2. ____________
3. ____________

4. ____________
5. ____________
6. ____________

B Complete with information about yourself. Use the games in Exercise A.

1. I like to play ____________.
2. I don't know how to play ____________.
3. As a child, I played ____________ with my friends.
4. ____________ is popular in my country.

C Unscramble each word. What is the game or toy?

1. noesmido dominoes
2. ckcheers ____________
3. hessc ____________
4. llod ____________
5. dacrs ____________
6. diec ____________
7. zzupel ____________
8. yonrcsa ____________

CD 2
Track 54

D Listen and complete.

jack	spades
queen	diamonds
king	clubs
ace	hearts

1. king of ____________
2. ____________ of ____________
3. ____________ of ____________
4. ____________ of ____________
5. ____________ of ____________
6. ____________ of ____________
7. ____________ of ____________
8. ____________ of ____________
9. ____________ of ____________

Grammar Connection: *I like to / I liked to*

Present	Past
I **like to** play cards.	I **liked to** play cards.
I **don't like to** play cards.	I **didn't like to** play cards.

E Do you like this activity? Complete each sentence with *I like to* or *I don't like to.*

1. ________________________________ knit.
2. ________________________________ embroider.
3. ________________________________ play cards.
4. ________________________________ crochet.
5. ________________________________ play chess.
6. ________________________________ play dominoes.

Did you like the activity when you were a child? Complete each sentence with *I liked to* or *I didn't like to.*

7. ________________________________ color with crayons.
8. ________________________________ play with dolls
9. ________________________________ put puzzles together
10. ________________________________ play cards
11. ________________________________ build models
12. ________________________________ play checkers

Camera, Stereo, and DVD

A Write the words for the electronic equipment in this living room.

~~television~~	dock	stereo
game system	speaker	DVD player
remote control	camera	DVD

1. television
2. ______
3. ______
4. ______
5. ______
6. ______
7. ______
8. ______
9. ______

B Write each word in the correct group.

camcorder	stereo	DVD	CD
~~camera~~	speaker	TV	zoom lens
MP3 player	tripod	satellite dish	boom box

Music	Movies / Programs	Photography
		camera

Grammar Connection: *But*

I have a camera,	**but**	I don't have a zoom lens.
She has an MP3 player,	**but**	she doesn't have headphones.

C **Complete the sentences.**

1. I have a camera, but I ___don't have___ a tripod.
2. My brother has a stereo, but he ________________ speakers.
3. I have a TV, but I ________________ a remote control.
4. My sister has a CD player, but she ________________ any CDs.
5. I have a TV, but I ________________ a game system.
6. They have a DVD player, but they ________________ any DVDs.

CD 2
Track 55

D **What equipment would each person like? Write the number of each statement with the correct item.**

________ a. headphones

________ b. boom box

________ c. stereo system

____1____ d. camcorder

________ e. video game system

________ f. camera

________ g. satellite dish

E **Look at the pictures on pages 226 and 227. Write two items you have in your home. Then, write two items you would like to have.**

1. I have a ________________ and a ________________.
2. I'd like a ________________ and a ________________.

Holidays and Celebrations

A Write the word for the holiday or celebration.

Halloween	Christmas	a birthday
Independence Day	~~Thanksgiving~~	Valentine's Day

1. Thanksgiving

2. ______

3. ______

4. ______

5. ______

6. ______

B Complete each sentence with the correct holiday or celebration.

Halloween	~~anniversary~~	retirement	Mother's Day
baby shower	Thanksgiving	New Year	Valentine's Day

1. Dennis and Marie got married ten years ago. They are celebrating their tenth anniversary.
2. Lee is 65 years old and he is leaving his company. His coworkers are giving him a ______ party.
3. Many countries celebrate the ______ with fireworks and parades.
4. On ______, children wear costumes.
5. Leena is expecting a baby next month. Her friends are giving her a ______.
6. On ______, children give their mothers gifts and cards.
7. Americans eat turkey and pumpkin pie on ______.
8. Husbands and wives say "I love you" on ______.

CD 2
Track 56

C **Listen to each statement or song. Which holiday or event are the people celebrating?**

1. a retirement
2. ______
3. ______
4. ______
5. ______
6. ______
7. ______
8. ______

Mother's Day
New Year
a birthday
Thanksgiving
Valentine's Day
Christmas
~~a retirement~~

Grammar Connection: Future Tense – *be going to*

I	am	going to	celebrate.
You They	are	going to	have a party.
She	is	going to	retire.

D **Choose the correct verb. Complete the sentences in the future tense.**

cook	~~wear~~	watch
celebrate	give	send

1. The children are going to wear costumes on Halloween.
2. She ______ a turkey for Thanksgiving.
3. We ______ the fireworks on Independence Day.
4. He ______ his girlfriend a card for Valentine's Day.
5. They ______ their tenth wedding anniversary tomorrow.
6. Leena's friends ______ her a baby shower.

Word Study

Take a few minutes each day to try to think in English. As you look at things, think of the words in English. Make sentences about the people, places, or things you see. For example, at the park you might think, "There are some ducks in the pond." or "I'm walking on the path."

Audioscript

Unit 1: Basic Words

Numbers *page 3*

F. Listen and write the floor and the room number.

1. Mr. Aker's office is on the fourth floor in Room 7.
2. Mrs. Brown's office is on the second floor in Room 5.
3. Dr. Chin's office is on the seventh floor in Room 21.
4. Mr. Dean's office is on the first floor in Room 4.
5. Mr. Edgar's office is on the third floor in Room 9.
6. Mrs. Franco's office is on the eighth floor in Room 1.

Time *page 5*

E. Listen to Henry's schedule. Write the time under each picture.

1. Henry gets up at 7:00.
2. He eats breakfast at 7:30.
3. He leaves the house at 8:15.
4. Henry gets to work at 9:00.
5. He gets home at 5:45.
6. Henry goes to bed at 11:30.

Calendar *page 7*

F. Listen and write the day you hear.

1. Today is Wednesday.
2. Tomorrow is Thursday.
3. Monday is a holiday.
4. School begins on Tuesday.
5. Do we have school on Friday?
6. I work on Saturday.
7. I don't work on Sunday.
8. My birthday is on Wednesday.
9. The party is on Saturday.
10. I'll see you on Thursday.

Money and Shopping *page 9*

D. Listen and write the amount. Use the cent or dollar symbol.

a. twenty-five cents
b. five cents
c. ten cents
d. one cent
e. fifty cents
f. five dollars
g. twenty dollars
h. one hundred dollars
i. one dollar
j. ten dollars

Colors *page 11*

C. Listen and write the number of each conversation under the correct picture.

1. A: That's my hat.
   B: Which one?
   A: The blue one.
2. A: That's my hat.
   B: Which one?
   A: The green one.
3. A: That's my hat.
   B: Which one?
   A: The black one.
4. A: That's my hat.
   B: Which one?
   A: The yellow one.
5. A: That's my hat.
   B: Which one?
   A: The red one.
6. A: That's my hat.
   B: Which one?
   A: The purple one.
7. A: That's my hat.
   B: Which one?
   A: The orange one.
8. A: That's my hat.
   B: Which one?
   A: The brown one.

In, On, Under *page 13*

D. Listen and write the number of each sentence under the correct picture.

1. The ball is to the right of the box.
2. The ball is between the boxes.
3. The ball is in the box.
4. The ball is behind the box.
5. The ball is in front of the box.
6. The ball is to the left of the box.
7. The ball is on the box.
8. The ball is under the box.

Opposites *page 15*

D. Listen to the questions. Circle *Yes* or *No*.

1. Is he young?
2. Is the house small?
3. Is she dirty?
4. Is he thin?
5. Are the windows open?
6. Is the glass empty?
7. Is the hat soft?
8. Is the building tall?

The Telephone *page 17*

D. Listen to each question. What is each person asking about?

1. What's the number for emergency assistance?
2. What's your phone number?
3. What's the number for information?
4. What's your area code?
5. What time zone are you in?

Unit 2: School

Classroom *page 19*

E. Look at the classroom in your dictionary. Listen and circle the correct answer.

1. Where's the clock?
2. Where's the marker?
3. Where's the overhead projector?
4. Where's the teacher?
5. Where's the poster?
6. Where's the globe?
7. Where's the alphabet?
8. Where's the homework assignment?
9. Where are the students?

Listen, Read, Write *page 21*

D. Listen to each sentence. Write the number of the sentence under the correct picture.

1. Erase the board.
2. Sit down.
3. Listen to a CD.
4. Close your book.
5. Share a book.
6. Write your name.
7. Raise your hand.
8. Look up the word in your dictionary.

School *page 23*

D. Listen to this student talk about his school. Match each room number with the correct room or person.

1. This is Room 101. It's the principal's office. The principal is in her office today.
2. Room 104 is the office of the guidance counselor.
3. Here's Room 120. It's a classroom.
4. This is Room 202. It's my favorite room. It's the cafeteria.
5. Room 206 is the library. The library is busy all day.
6. If a student feels sick, she can see the nurse. Her office is in Room 209.
7. Room 215 is the teachers' lounge. The teachers eat and talk here.
8. Room 301 is the language lab. I use the language lab two days a week.

Computers *page 25*

D. Listen to the sentences. Write the word you hear.

1. I am using a scanner.
2. He has a laptop.
3. The projector is on the table.
4. Send me an e-mail.
5. Press the Enter key.
6. Click on that icon.
7. Put the CD-ROM in the computer.
8. There is paper in the printer.

Unit 3: Family

Family *page 27*

D. Look at the family in Exercise C and listen to the questions. Circle the correct answers.

1. Who is Jim's wife?
2. Who is Jacob's father?
3. Who is Mary's daughter?
4. Who is Sarah's husband?
5. Who is Jacob's sister?
6. Who is Tommy's brother?
7. Who is Larry's son?
8. Who is Tony's grandmother?
9. Who is Jacob's cousin?
10. Who is Ed's niece?

Raising a Child *page 29*

E. Listen to each sentence. Write the number of each sentence under the correct picture.

1. Encourage your child.
2. Put your child to bed.
3. Help your child.
4. Drop your child off at school.
5. Pick your child up.
6. Praise your child.

Life Events *page 31*

E. Listen to the life of John Lennon. Match the dates and the events.

1. John Lennon is born in 1940.
2. In 1961, he starts the Beatles with three friends.
3. He and Cynthia Powell get married in 1962.
4. In 1963, he and his wife have a baby, Julian.
5. In 1964, the Beatles travel to the United States.
6. In 1968, he and Cynthia Powell get divorced.
7. In 1969, he marries Yoko Ono.
8. Also in 1969, he plays with the Beatles for the last time.
9. In 1975, he and Yoko have a baby, Sean.
10. In 1980, he dies in New York.

Unit 4: People

Face and Hair *page 32*

C. Listen and write the letter of the correct man.

1. He has glasses.
2. He has a beard.
3. He has a moustache.
4. He has black hair.
5. He's bald.
6. He has gray hair.

Daily Activities *page 35*

E. Listen. Circle the correct answer.

1. What time do you wake up?
2. Do you take a shower in the morning?
3. Do you eat lunch every day?
4. When do you go to work?
5. Do you take a nap in the afternoon?
6. When do you do the housework?
7. Do you eat dinner with your family?
8. Do you work out?
9. When do you watch television?
10. What time do you go to bed?

Walk, Jump, Run *page 37*

D. Look at the picture. Listen to each question and write the name of the correct person.

1. Who is running?
2. Who is sitting down?
3. Who is getting off the bus?
4. Who is entering the school?
5. Who is going up the stairs?
6. Who is getting out of the car?
7. Who is jumping rope?
8. Who is walking to school?
9. Who is crossing the street?

Feelings *page 39*

E. Listen. How does each person feel?

1. Oh! Excuse me! I'm so sorry!
2. Just stop talking about it!
3. My son is the best soccer player in his class.
4. I had a whole pizza! I ate too much!
5. Where is she? It's midnight. I'm going to call the police.
6. Really? Grandma is getting married?!
7. I feel terrible! I have a headache and my stomach hurts. I'm going to bed.
8. We have a big test today.
9. This is my favorite chair. I like to put my feet up and relax in it.
10. Jack! Wake up! I think I hear someone in the house!

Wave, Greet, Smile *page 41*

D. Listen to each sentence. Write the number of the sentence under the correct picture.

1. A man and woman are dancing.
2. Two businessmen are shaking hands.
3. A boy and girl are smiling.
4. A man is waving goodbye.
5. A woman is bowing.
6. A father is hugging his daughter.

Documents *page 43*

E. Read the list of documents. Listen and write the number of each request next to the correct document.

1. Sir, let me see your driver's license.
2. Do you have a business card?
3. We need a copy of your high school diploma.
4. You need your student ID to borrow a library book.
5. Do you have a green card?
6. Your passport, please.
7. I need a copy of your marriage certificate.
8. Where is the vehicle registration card?

Nationalities *page 45*

D. Listen and complete the sentences.

1. Some Thai food is spicy.
2. Many Greek desserts are very sweet.
3. The Hermitage is a famous Russian museum.
4. Malaysian beaches are popular with tourists.
5. Shogatsu is the Japanese New Year.
6. Colombian coffee is delicious.
7. Egyptian history is very interesting.

Unit 5: Community

Places Around Town *page 47*

E. Listen. Where is each person? Write the place.

1. He's reading a book at the library.
2. She's parking her car in the parking garage.
3. They're watching a good movie at the movie theater.
4. She's visiting her sister in the hospital.
5. He's shopping at the mall.
6. They're staying at the motel.
7. They're working at the factory.
8. They're watching a baseball game at the stadium.
9. He's looking for a car at the car dealership.
10. He's getting gas at the gas station.

Shops and Stores *page 49*

D. Listen to each shopper. Complete each sentence with the correct shop or store.

1. I'd like ten copies of this form.
2. A large vanilla ice cream cone, please.
3. I have a prescription from my doctor.
4. I'm here for my hair appointment with Sonia.
5. A dozen red roses, please.
6. A loaf of bread and an apple pie, please.
7. Do you have any exercise classes in the evenings?
8. The name is Simmons. I'm picking up my shirts and suits.
9. Do you have Gloria Estefan's newest CD?

Bank *page 51*

D. Listen and circle the correct answer.

1. Do you have a checking account?
2. Where are your important documents?
3. Where are the safe-deposit boxes?
4. How much interest do you receive on your account?
5. What's your checking account number?
6. What's your balance?
7. How do you pay your telephone bill?
8. Do you have a bankcard?

Post Office *page 53*

E. Listen to each statement. Write the word you hear.

1. Write a letter.
2. Put it in an envelope.
3. Write the mailing address.
4. Don't forget the zip code.
5. Write your return address.
6. Now you need a stamp.
7. Put the letter in the mailbox.

Library *page 55*

D. Listen to each statement. Write the word you hear.

1. Shakespeare is a famous author.
2. What's today's headline?
3. Nelson Mandela's autobiography is very interesting.
4. You can find maps of South America in the atlas.
5. Here's my library card.
6. What's the title of the book?
7. You can read quietly in the reading room.
8. The librarian can help you find that information.

Daycare Center *page 57*

E. Listen as Mrs. Chin talks to her babysitter. Write the number of the item you hear under the correct picture.

1. Put the baby in his high chair at 6:00 and give him his dinner.
2. He needs a bib. The bibs are here on the counter.
3. Give him a bottle at about 7:00.
4. There's a changing table in his bedroom.
5. You'll see the box of disposable diapers.
6. Put the dirty diaper in the diaper pail.
7. Put him in his crib at about 7:30.
8. When you put him to bed, give him a pacifier.

City Square *page 59*

D. Listen. Where is each person? Write the place.

1. Two tickets for the van Gogh exhibit, please.
2. I'd like a cup of coffee.
3. How much is this newspaper?
4. I'd like to take a trip to Mexico.
5. I need a room for three nights.
6. I'd like to buy some traveler's checks.
7. Where is the bus station?

Crime and Justice *page 61*

D. Listen and complete the sentences with the word or words you hear.

1. The police arrested a woman for murder.
2. A man is on trial for arson.
3. The police stopped a woman for drunk driving.
4. The woman is in prison for armed robbery.
5. He is in jail for auto theft.
6. The store stopped the woman for shoplifting.
7. The man is in jail for drug dealing.
8. The police arrested them for bribery.

Unit 6: Housing

Types of Homes *page 63*

C. Read the list of words. Listen to each statement. Write the word you hear.

1. My parents live in an apartment in the city.
2. My sister lives in a ranch in the country.
3. My brother lives in a mobile home in a small town.
4. My cousin lives in a farmhouse in the country.
5. I live in a house in the suburbs.
6. My neighbors live in a duplex.
7. My friend lives in a condominium.
8. My grandparents live in a retirement home in a small town.

Finding a Place to Live *page 65*

E. Listen to each conversation. Write the number of the conversation under the correct picture.

1. Man: We'd like to apply for a loan.
   Banker: How much would you like to borrow?
   Man: $100,000.
2. Woman: Let's look at some houses in the area.
   Man: Okay. I'll call a real estate agent.
3. Seller: The price is $110,000.
   Realtor: We'd like to negotiate the price. My client is offering $105,000.
4. Banker: Mr. and Mrs. Young, the bank has approved your loan.
   Woman: Great.
   Banker: You will need to sign these loan documents. Sign here, and here, . . .
5. Woman: The movers are coming tomorrow.
   Man: We're moving some things ourselves.
6. Realtor: This house has three bedrooms.
   Man: We'd like to look at it.
7. Woman: The house is old. Is everything OK?
   Man: Yes. I inspected everything. The house is in good condition.
8. Woman: Here it is. We're making our first house payment.
   Man: Yes. Thirty more years of house payments!

Apartment Building *page 66*

C. Listen to this conversation between a landlord and a person looking for an apartment. Put a check (✓) next to the features the apartment has. Put an *X* next to the features the apartment doesn't have.

A: This is the apartment for rent. It's a one-bedroom apartment.
B: It's very hot in here. Does the apartment have an air conditioner?
A: No, it doesn't have an air conditioner.
B: Does the apartment have a balcony?
A: No, but it has a fire escape. You can sit on the fire escape.
B: Is the neighborhood safe?
A: Don't worry. Each apartment has a dead-bolt lock and a peephole.
B: Does the building have a laundry room?
A: No, it doesn't.
B: How about parking? Does each apartment have a parking space?
A: No, it doesn't. You can park on the street.
B: This building is on the fourth floor. Does the building have an elevator?
A: No, it doesn't have an elevator. There are only five floors. It doesn't need an elevator.
B: Sorry. I'm not interested in this apartment!

House and Garden *page 69*

E. Look at the pictures of the two houses. Listen to each statement. Does it describe House A or House B?

1. This house has a porch.
2. There is a fence in front of this house.
3. This house has a chimney.
4. There is a sprinkler in front of this house.
5. There is a garden on the side of this house.
6. There is a wheelbarrow in the garden.
7. This house has a garage.
8. This house has two skylights.
9. This house has a hammock in the side yard.
10. The windows of this house have shutters.
11. There is a grill in the side yard.
12. The front door is open.

Kitchen and Dining Area *page 71*

D. Look at the two place settings. Listen to each statement. Does it describe place setting A, place setting B, or both?

1. There is a plate on the table.
2. There is a bowl on the plate.
3. There is a napkin on the table.
4. There is no silverware on the table.
5. There is a placemat on the table.
6. There is a teapot on the table.
7. There is a mug next to the teapot.
8. There is a glass on the table.
9. There is a candle on the table.
10. There is silverware on the table.

Living Room *page 73*

D. Listen to the conversations. Write the number of each conversation under the correct picture.

1. A: It's really cold in here.
   B: It is. Let's start a fire in the fireplace.
2. A: I am so tired!
   B: Sit in the armchair. It's very comfortable.
3. A: I'm looking for my book.
   B: Oh! I put it in the bookcase.
4. A: Are you hot?
   B: Yes. I'll turn on the ceiling fan.
5. A: Where is the light switch?
   B: It's over there, on the wall.
6. A: Jack, look. The dog is on the sofa again.
   B: Rex, get off the sofa!
7. A: Laura, I can't find my glasses.
   B: Look on the end table.
8. A: It's too bright in here.
   B: Put down the blinds.

Bedroom and Bathroom *page 75*

E. Listen to the parent's instructions. Write the number of each sentence under the correct picture.

1. Empty the wastebasket.
2. The water is still running. Turn off the faucet.
3. Go into the bathroom and take a shower.
4. Put a new roll of toilet paper in the bathroom.
5. Hang up your towel.
6. Please make your bed.
7. Hang your coat in the closet.
8. Set your alarm clock for 6:30.

Household Problems *page 77*

D. Listen to each problem. Who is each person talking to?

1. A: Hello.
   B: Hello. My name is Mrs. Johnson. I have a problem with my toilet. The toilet is clogged.
   A: We can come and look at it tomorrow.
2. A: Hello.
   B: This is Mr. Chen. We have mice in the kitchen. Lots of mice.
   A: No problem. We can come this afternoon.
3. A: Good morning.
   B: Good morning. My name is Ms. Perez. I have a problem with my front door. The lock is jammed. I can't open it.
   A: I'm very busy today. I can come tomorrow morning.
4. A: Good morning.
   B: Hello. This is Mr. O'Brian. Our roof is leaking.
   A: I can look at it on Friday.
5. A: Hello.
   B: Hello. My name is Kara Longo. The power in our house is out. We have no electricity.
   A: I can come over right now.
6. A: Hello.
   B: Hello. This is Mrs. Orwell. The window in our kitchen is broken. Can you fix it some day this week?
   A: No problem. I can fix it on Wednesday.
7. A: Good afternoon.
   B: Good afternoon. My name is George Young. The basement is flooded. We have a lot of water on the floor.
   A: I can come over in an hour.

Household Chores *page 79*

E. Listen to a mother talk with her children. Draw a line from each child to the chores the mother gives him.

Mom: Okay, boys. It's Saturday morning and it's time to clean the house.
Mom: Jason, vacuum the carpets in all the rooms—the living room, the dining room, and all the bedrooms. Then, polish the furniture.
Jason: Okay.
Mom: Kevin, do the dishes. Then, mop the floor in the kitchen.
Kevin: Okay, Mom.
Mom: Mike, empty the wastebaskets. All the waste-baskets in the house.
Mike: No problem.
Mom: Then, mow the grass.
Mike: Mom! Dad always mows the grass.
Mom: I know. But Dad's working today. So, mow the grass.
Mike: Oh, okay.

Cleaning Supplies *page 81*

C. Listen to each conversation. Write the item that each family needs.

1. A: Please turn on the dishwasher.
   B: We don't have any dishwasher detergent.
2. A: Please vacuum the carpet.
   B: We don't have any vacuum cleaner bags.
3. A: Please wash the dishes.
   B: We don't have any dish soap.
4. A: Oh! We have a mouse!
   B: And we don't have any mousetraps.
5. A: Please wash the windows.
   B: We don't have any glass cleaner.
6. A: Please empty the garbage.
   B: Okay. But we need more garbage bags.
7. A: Please polish the furniture.
   B: We don't have any furniture polish.
8. A: Please wash the dirty pots and pans.
   B: I can't. We don't have any scouring pads.
9. A: Get that fly!
   B: Where is the flyswatter?

Unit 7: Food

Fruits and Nuts *page 83*

D. Listen to each conversation. Which fruit is each speaker talking about?

1. A: Do you like apple pie?
   B: I love apple pie.
2. A: Would you like a pear?
   B: Yes, thanks.
3. A: Do we have any grapes?
   B: Yes. They're in the refrigerator.
4. A: What would you like in your tea?
   B: Lemon, please.
5. A: Do you put nuts in your salads?
   B: Sometimes I put walnuts in a salad.
6. A: What kind of fruit is this?
   B: It's a pomegranate.
7. A: What's your favorite kind of ice cream?
   B: I like strawberry ice cream.
8. A: Is an avocado a fruit?
   B: Yes, it's a fruit.
9. A: Do you like kiwis?
   B: Not really.
10. A: Do we have any olives?
    B: No, I need to buy some.

Vegetables *page 85*

D. Look at the ad above and listen for the price of each item. Write the price of the item in the box below the vegetable.

Asparagus is $4.99 a pound.
Spinach is $2.39 a pound.
Mushrooms are $3.50 a pound.
Celery is $2.50 each.
Artichokes are $1.50 each.
Cabbage is 59 cents a pound.
Peas are $2.99 a pound.
Scallions are $1.59 a bunch.
Potatoes are $1.39 a pound.

Meat, Poultry, and Seafood *page 87*

E. Listen and complete.

1. A: Can I help you?
   B: Two pounds of ground beef, please.
2. A: Next!
   B: A small piece of tuna.
3. A: Yes, ma'am?
   B: Four chicken legs, please.
4. A: Can I help you?
   B: A large roast beef, please.
5. A: Yes, sir.
   B: Six pork chops.
6. A: Who's next?
   B: I am! Three chicken breasts.
7. A: Can I help you?
   B: One pound of shrimp.
8. A: Yes?
   B: Two veal cutlets.
9. A: And how can I help you today?
   B: A chicken, please. Let's see. It's for six people, so a six or seven pound chicken.
10. A: Next!
    B: A small pork roast.

Inside the Refrigerator *page 89*

D. Listen to the conversation between the man and the woman. Circle the items they need at the store. Cross out the items they don't need.

A: What do we need at the store?
B: We need milk.
A: Okay. Milk.
B: And ice cream.
A: What flavor?
B: Vanilla.
A: How about eggs?
B: No, we don't need eggs.
A: Cheese? Do we have cheese?
B: Yes, we have cheese. We need salad dressing.
A: What kind of salad dressing?
B: Italian.
A: And soda?
B: No, don't buy soda. But, get some bottled water.
A: Do we have butter?
B: Yes, we have butter. But we need margarine.
A: Okay. Anything else?
B: Get some more frozen vegetables.
A: Okay. Is that all?
B: I think so.

Food to Go *page 91*

C. Listen and write the number of each order under the correct picture.

1. A: Your order?
   B: A small pizza.
   A: What kind?
   B: Just a regular cheese pizza.
2. A: Can I help you?
   B: A cup of coffee and a doughnut.
   A: What kind of doughnut?
   B: A sugar doughnut.
3. A: Are you ready to order?
   B: Lasagna, please.
   A: Anything else?
   B: A soda, please.
4. A: Can I take your order?
   B: Sushi, please.
   A: And to drink?
   B: Tea.
5. A: Can I help you?
   B: A hamburger and french fries.
   A: And to drink?
   B: A soda.
   A: Large?
   B: No, medium.
6. A: Your order, please?
   B: The fish and chips.
   A: Anything to drink?
   B: Water, please.

Cooking *page 93*

C. Listen and complete the recipe.

1. Scramble the eggs in a bowl.
2. Chop the onion and the pepper.
3. Grate the cheese.
4. Slice and dice the ham.
5. Grease the frying pan with the butter.
6. Cook the eggs for a few minutes.
7. Add the onion, pepper, cheese, and ham.
8. Cook the eggs for three more minutes.
9. Fold the omelette and serve immediately.

Cooking Equipment *page 95*

D. Two cooks are working together in a kitchen. Listen and complete the sentences.

1. Please get the ladle.
2. I need a knife.
3. Do we have a wok?
4. Please hand me the strainer.
5. Where's the timer?
6. I can't find the peeler.
7. Do we have a grater?
8. Please give me the spatula.
9. We need a whisk.
10. Use the steamer.

Measurements and Containers *page 97*

E. Listen and write the number of each statement or question under the correct item.

1. Let's buy that bouquet of flowers.
2. The tomatoes in that basket look delicious.
3. There's a pitcher of milk in the refrigerator.
4. Let's buy a jar of tomato sauce.
5. Would you like a piece of chocolate cake?
6. There's a pile of oranges on the counter.

Supermarket *page 99*

E. Listen to the questions. Check the correct section of the supermarket.

1. A: Where is the butter?
   B: It's in the dairy section.
2. A: Where is the ice cream?
   B: It's in the frozen foods section.
3. A: Where is the ground beef?
   B: It's in the meat and poultry section.
4. A: Where can I get cold cuts?
   B: They're in the deli.
5. A: Where are the apples?
   B: They're in the produce section.
6. A: Where are the eggs?
   B: They're in the dairy section.
7. A: Where is the bread?
   B: It's in the bakery.
8. A: Where are the tomatoes?
   B: They're in the produce section.

Restaurant *page 101*

E. Listen and draw each item in the correct place on this table.

1. The plate is on the table.
2. Put the knife to the right of the plate.
3. Put the spoon next to the knife.
4. Put the napkin to the left of the plate.
5. Put the fork on the napkin.
6. Put the water glass above the knife and spoon.
7. Put the wine glass to the right of the water glass.
8. Put the bowl on the plate.
9. Put the saltshaker above the plate.
10. Put the pepper shaker next to the saltshaker.

Order, Eat, Pay *page 103*

C. Look at the restaurant in your dictionary. Listen to the statements and write the number of the server or customer.

a. A boy is looking at the menu.
b. A waitress is setting the table.
c. The children are sharing a dessert.
d. A waiter is offering a doggie bag.
e. A waitress is serving the meal.
f. A woman is making a reservation.
g. A waitress is lighting a candle.
h. A waiter is refilling the water.
i. A girl is spilling her drink.

Unit 8: Clothing

Clothes *page 105*

D. Look at the picture above and listen to each statement. Circle *True* or *False*.

1. Ali is wearing overalls.
2. Ali is wearing a hat.
3. Bonnie is wearing a raincoat.
4. Bonnie is wearing jeans.
5. Cara is wearing a shawl.
6. Cara is wearing a dress.
7. Dana is wearing a sweater.
8. Dana is wearing a blouse.
9. Ed is wearing a shirt.
10. Ed is wearing a jacket.

Sleepwear, Underwear, and Swimwear *page 107*

C. Look in your dictionary and listen to each statement. Write the number of the item you hear.

a. I always wear a white undershirt under my shirt.
b. My bathing suit is red with purple flowers.
c. When it is very cold, I wear long underwear.
d. I have green swimming trunks.
e. In the winter, I wear my long, pink nightgown.
f. In the summer, I wear flip flops to the beach.
g. I have warm, yellow slippers.
h. My purple nightshirt is on the clothesline.
i. I have an old, yellow bathrobe that I wear every night.

Shoes and Accessories *page 109*

E. Listen to each conversation. Write the number of the conversation under the correct picture.

1. A: What are you buying?
   B: A watch. My watch broke.
2. A: Do you like this necklace?
   B: Yes. It's pretty.
   A: I think I'll buy it.
3. A: I like these heels.
   B: They'll look great with your black dress.
4. A: What would you like for your birthday?
   B: A belt. A black belt.
5. A: What are you looking for?
   B: A hat. I need a knit hat.
6. A: I lost my sunglasses.
   B: There's a sale on sunglasses at the drugstore.
7. A: I'm looking for long silver earrings.
   B: How about these earrings?
   A: They're nice.
8. A: How do you like this ring?
   B: It's beautiful!

Describing Clothes page 111

D. Look at the people in Exercise C. Listen to each question and write the name of the correct person.

1. Who is wearing high heels?
2. Who is wearing straight leg jeans?
3. Who is wearing a turtleneck?
4. Who is wearing a tie?
5. Who is wearing a polo shirt?
6. Who is wearing baggy pants?
7. Who is wearing a short skirt?
8. Who is wearing a V-neck sweater?

Fabrics and Patterns page 113

E. Listen to each conversation and look at the ties in Exercise D. Write the letter of the correct tie.

1. A: Which tie should I wear?
   B: Wear the striped tie with that shirt.
2. A: Do you like this tie?
   B: Yes. I like the print tie with that shirt.
3. A: Do you like this tie?
   B: No. Wear a solid tie with that shirt.
4. A: Which tie looks better?
   B: I think the polka dot one. Yes, definitely the polka dot one.
5. A: Which tie do you like?
   B: Let's see. The floral one looks nice.
6. A: Do you like the checked tie with this shirt?
   B: Yes, the checked tie looks good.
7. A: Do you like this paisley tie?
   B: Yes. That shirt looks good with the paisley tie.
8. A: Which tie should I wear?
   B: With that shirt, wear the plaid tie.

Buying, Wearing, and Caring for Clothes page 115

D. Listen and write the word or phrase you hear.

1. Mom, can we go shopping?
2. Dad, can I buy this shirt?
3. Mom, can you unzip my jacket?
4. Dad, can I try on these jeans?
5. Mom, can you wash my pants?
6. Dad, can you mend my jacket?
7. Mom, can you sew on my button?
8. Dad, can you iron my shirt?

Sewing and Laundry page 117

E. Charles does the laundry on Saturday morning. Listen and put the steps you hear in order.

I wash my clothes every Saturday morning. First, I separate the dark clothes and the light clothes. Then, I turn on the washing machine. I add the laundry detergent and the bleach, then, I put the clothes in the machine. There's a little cup on the side of the machine, and I put the fabric softener in that cup. When the machine goes off, I put the wet clothes in the dryer and turn it on. When the clothes are dry, I put them in the laundry basket.

Unit 9: Transportation

Vehicles and Traffic Signs page 119

C. Listen and complete each sentence.

1. My cousin lives in the mountains. He drives an SUV.
2. My mother drives her convertible with the top down.
3. My father works at a gas station. He drives a tow truck.
4. My grandparents like to travel in their RV.
5. My cousin has a farm. He needs a pickup.
6. My aunt works for a school. She drives a school bus.
7. My girlfriend wears a helmet when she rides her motorcycle.
8. My sister has three children. She loves her minivan.
9. My brother makes large deliveries. He drives a tractor trailer.
10. My friend drives to work in his compact car.

Parts of a Car page 121

E. Listen to each car problem. Circle the part of the car you hear.

1. I turn on the air conditioning, but only hot air comes out.
2. The right turn signal doesn't work.
3. The left headlight is out.
4. The horn doesn't work.
5. The battery is dead.
6. These wipers are old. I need new windshield wipers.
7. The speedometer doesn't work.
8. The oil gauge says I have no oil, but I put oil in the car last week.
9. I have a flat tire.
10. Please check the radiator. My car overheats when it's hot.

Road Trip page 123

E. Last summer Tony and Maria went on vacation to the mountains. Listen and write the number of each sentence under the correct picture.

1. Tony and Maria packed.
2. Then, they left on their vacation.
3. They got gas.
4. Then, they got on the highway.
5. They drove 200 miles.
6. They paid the toll.
7. The got off the highway.
8. Tony and Maria arrived at the mountains.

Airport *page 125*

E. Listen to each statement. Write the word you hear.

1. I need to see your photo ID.
2. You have to go through immigration.
3. Your plane leaves from Gate 21.
4. You can take one carry-on bag.
5. I'd like economy class.
6. There are four emergency exits on this plane.
7. The flight attendant is serving soda and juice.
8. The Fasten Your Seat Belt sign is on.

Taking a Flight *page 127*

E. Listen to each airport worker. What does the passenger need to do?

1. I need to see your photo ID.
2. Your flight will leave from Gate 42.
3. Please fasten your seat belts.
4. Please turn off your cell phones.
5. We are now serving lunch.
6. Your can pick up your bags in the baggage claim area.

Public Transportation *page 128*

C. Listen to these students talk about how they get to school. Complete the chart.

1. A: Natalia, how do you get to school?
   B: I take the bus. The bus stop is across the street from my house.
   A: How much is the fare?
   B: It's $2.00. I use a token.
2. A: Adam, how do you get to school?
   B: I take the subway.
   A: How much is the fare?
   B: It's $1.50. I have a fare card.
3. A: Lin, how do you get to school?
   B: I take the ferry.
   A: How much is the fare?
   B: It's $2.00.
4. A: Salim, how do you get to school?
   B: I take the train.
   A: How much is the fare?
   B: It's $5.00.
5. A: Francisco, how do you get to school?
   B: I take the bus.
   A: How much is it?
   B: It's a dollar.

Up, Over, Around *page 131*

C. Listen and complete the directions.

Let me tell you about my ride to school.

1. First, I go over a bridge.
2. Then, I go through a park.
3. I go past a big church.
4. After that, I go along a river.
5. I go around a curve.
6. Then, I go through a tunnel.
7. I go across a railroad crossing.
8. I go into the parking lot.
9. I walk across the street.
10. I go into the school building.

Unit 10: Health

The Human Body *page 133*

D. Listen and complete these sentences. Then draw a line from each sentence to the correct picture.

1. Bend at the waist.
2. Raise your hand.
3. Stand on one foot.
4. Touch your toes.
5. Put your hands on your head.
6. Put your hands on your hips.
7. Touch your elbows to your knees.

Illnesses, Injuries, Symptoms, and Disabilities *page 135*

C. Listen to each conversation. Circle the problem.

1. A: I feel terrible.
   B: What's the problem?
   A: I have the flu.
2. A: I don't feel well.
   B: What's the matter?
   A: I have a bad stomachache.
3. A: I'm going home.
   B: Why?
   A: I have an earache.
4. A: I feel sick.
   B: What's the matter?
   A: I don't know. I feel dizzy.
5. A: Can I leave class early?
   B: Are you sick?
   A: Yes. I have a fever.
6. A: I don't feel well.
   B: What's the matter?
   A: I have a really bad headache.
7. A: I can't write.
   B: Why not?
   A: I have a sprained wrist.
8. A: My son is home from school today.
   B: Is he sick?
   A: Yes. He has the mumps.
9. A: I feel terrible.
   B: What's the matter?
   A: I have a sore throat.
10. A: My husband is home from work today.
    B: Is he sick?
    A: Yes, he has a bad backache.

Hurting and Healing *page 137*

E. Listen to each emergency phone call. Circle the emergency.

1. A: Emergency assistance.
   B: Send an ambulance. I think my mother is having a heart attack.
2. A: Emergency assistance.
   B: My son broke a window and cut his arm very badly.
3. A: Emergency assistance.
   B: There was a bad accident in front of my house. The driver is unconscious.
4. A: Emergency assistance.
   B: Please help! My child just swallowed poison.
5. A: Emergency assistance.
   B: Come quickly. There's a man in the river. I think he's drowning.
6. A: Emergency assistance.
   B: My daughter was stung by a bee. She's having an allergic reaction.
7. A: Emergency assistance.
   B: My friend is on the floor. I think she overdosed on drugs.

Hospital *page 139*

E. Listen and complete the statements.

1. We need to take an x-ray of your arm.
2. Press the call button if you need a nurse.
3. You need ten stitches.
4. Your operation is Friday at 7:00 A.M.
5. My brother is in the intensive care unit.
6. The orderly will take you to your room.
7. Do you know how to do CPR?
8. Can you bring me a bedpan?
9. I need to take some blood from your arm.
10. She's an excellent surgeon.

Medical Center *page 141*

E. What kind of doctor is each person talking to?

1. I have a cavity.
2. I have a pain in my chest.
3. I can't see the board in class.
4. I think I'm pregnant.
5. I feel sad all the time.
6. My son needs his immunizations for school.
7. I need a physical for work.
8. I think my daughter broke her hand.
9. I have a backache.

Pharmacy *page 143*

E. Listen to each conversation between a pharmacist and a customer. What does the pharmacist recommend?

1: A: Can I help you?
   B: Yes, I have a sore throat.
   A: Try some throat lozenges.
2. A: Can I help you?
   B: I have a bad headache.
   A: You need aspirin.
3. A: Yes? Can I help you?
   B: My son sprained his wrist.
   A: Use an elastic bandage on his wrist.
4. A: Yes? Can I help you?
   B: My eyes are red.
   A: Try these eye drops.
5. A: Can I help you?
   B: Yes. I'm having pains in my chest.
   A: You need to go to the hospital.
6. A: Can I help you?
   B: I have an infection. I think I need an antibiotic.
   A: You need to see a doctor. You need a prescription.
7. A: Yes? Can I help you?
   B: I have a backache.
   A: Try a heating pad.
8. A: Can I help you?
   B: My son has a stuffy nose.
   A: Try a humidifier in his room. That will help.

Soap, Comb, and Floss *page 145*

D. Listen to the advertisements. Write the number of each advertisement under the correct picture.

1. Keep your hair clean and shiny all day. Use Dell Shampoo.
2. Enjoy a smooth, refreshing shave. Buy Aloe Shaving Cream.
3. Feel dry and secure all day. Try Always Deodorant.
4. Protect your skin from the sun. Buy Sun Light SunScreen.
5. Smell as beautiful as you look. Use new Evening Song Perfume.
6. Get your teeth clean and white. Use Fresh Toothpaste.
7. Keep your skin smooth and young-looking. Buy Lamay Lotion.
8. Keep your hair in place all day. Try Gene's Hair Gel.

Unit 11: Work

Jobs 1 *page 147*

D. Listen and write the job you hear.

1. My uncle works in a factory. He's an assembler.
2. My cousin works in a school. He's a janitor.
3. My aunt works for a big company. She's a businesswoman.
4. My brother works in a nursing home. He's a health aide.
5. My sister works in a studio. She's an artist.
6. My friend works for a book company. He's an editor.
7. My mother works in a beauty salon. She's a hairstylist.
8. My father works in a supermarket. He's a butcher.
9. My friend acts in movies. He's an actor.
10. My sister works for a family in our area. She's a babysitter.

Jobs 2 *page 149*

E. Listen to the conversations. Circle the correct job.

1. A: What color nail polish would you like?
   B: I like this pink.
2. A: Is everybody ready?
   B: Yes!
   A: Look at the camera. Smile!
3. A: I need to see your license and registration.
   B: Why, officer?
   A: You were going 40 miles per hour. The speed limit is 25 miles per hour.
4. A: What countries would you like to visit?
   B: We'd like to visit Spain, France, and Italy.
5. A: Our cat isn't eating much. And he's getting very fat.
   B: Well, your cat isn't a he. It's a she. And she's having kittens.
6. A: That's a beautiful painting.
   B: Yes, this painting is by van Gogh. It's called *Starry Night.*
7. A: And now, our up-to-the-minute traffic report from Luis Lane.
   B: Traffic is very heavy this morning. There's a bad accident on Route 5 in Milltown. . . .
8. A: That jacket looks great on you!
   B: I don't know. I think it's too small.
   A: It's a size 10. Try a size 12.

Working *page 150*

B. Listen and match each person with the correct action.

1. A: Here's your package, sir. Please sign here.
   B: On the line?
   A: Yes.
2. A: I want Mommy.
   B: Sh. Sh. Don't cry. Mommy and daddy will be home soon.
3. A: Tops Trucking.
   B: This is Freddie. I can't come to work today. I feel terrible.
   A: Okay, Freddie. I'll tell the manager.
4. A: Tell me about this TV.
   B: This is our most popular TV. It has the best picture and sound.
   A: Okay. It *is* a great picture. I'll take it.
5. A: We think you are the best person for the job.
   B: Thank you.
   A: Can you start work on Monday?
   B: Monday? Yes, that's fine.
6. A: How many copies do you need?
   B: Ten copies, please.
   A: Okay.
7. A: Oh! Antonio, my love!
   B: Oh! Maria! At last, I am with you!

Farm *page 153*

E. Listen and circle the animal you hear.

1. [horse]
2. [rooster]
3. [dog]
4. [sheep]
5. [goat]
6. [cow]
7. [cat]
8. [chicken]
9. [donkey]
10. [pig]

Office *page 155*

E. Listen to each question. Write the number of each question under the correct item.

1. Can I use your stapler?
2. Can I have a paper clip?
3. Do you have any tape?
4. Do you have any rubber bands?
5. Can I have a thumbtack?
6. Can I use your pencil sharpener?
7. Do you have any sticky notes?
8. Do you have any staples?
9. Can I use your calculator for a few minutes?
10. Do you have a fax machine?
11. Do you have an extra folder?
12. Can I use your paper shredder?

Factory *page 157*

E. Listen and circle the word you hear.

1. Where's your hard hat?
2. We need more parts.
3. The conveyor belt is moving.
4. The robot isn't working.
5. Give this information to the shipping clerk.
6. I can't find my safety glasses.
7. Talk to the supervisor.
8. Put on your safety vest.

Hotel *page 159*

E. Listen to each hotel guest. Where is the guest? Circle the correct place in the hotel.

1. Do you sell postcards?
2. I'd like to check in.
3. This party is great!
4. I need my car at 2:00.
5. We can use the computers here.
6. I like to exercise here early in the morning.
7. Sorry I'm late for the meeting.
8. It's really hot in here!

Tools and Supplies 1 *page 160*

B. Look at the picture in Exercise A. Listen to each statement and circle *True* or *False*.

1. Brian is using a drill.
2. There's a file on the floor.
3. Brian is holding a wrench.
4. Brian is wearing a tool belt.
5. There's a ruler on the floor.
6. There's a screwdriver on the floor.
7. There's a level on the shelf.
8. Yoshi is using a power sander.
9. The wood is in the vise.
10. Yoshi is using an extension cord.
11. There's a router on the worktable.
12. There's a handsaw on the floor.

Tools and Supplies 2 *page 163*

E. Listen and write the number of the sentence you hear under the correct picture.

1. Please hand me the scraper.
2. This screw is loose. Do you have a screwdriver?
3. What color paint do you like?
4. We're going to put new tile in the bathroom.
5. I can't see. Where's the flashlight?
6. That paintbrush is too wide. Use a small paintbrush for the windows.

Drill, Sand, Paint *page 165*

C. Listen and circle the instructions you hear.

1. Plaster the drywall in the living room.
2. You can wire the house now.
3. Push the wheelbarrow over there.
4. Paint the wall in the bedroom.
5. Saw the wood carefully.
6. Pour the concrete for the sidewalk.
7. Drill a hole in that wall.
8. Tear down the drywall in the kitchen.

Unit 12: Earth and Space

Weather *page 167*

E. Listen to the weather report for the week. Draw the symbols to show the weather for each day. Then circle the word for the temperature.

And now, please listen for your weekly weather report.

Money is going to be the best day of the week for weather. Enjoy the sun and the warm temperatures.

It is going to rain on Tuesday and the temperatures are going to be cool.

On Wednesday, it's going to be cloudy. Wear your heavy winter coats for the cold temperatures.

It's going to be windy on Thursday. The cold temperatures are going to continue.

And on Friday, the snow is going to begin. There is going to be heavy snow all day. Expect freezing temperatures.

The Earth's Surface *page 168*

B. Look at the map in Exercise A and listen to each sentence. Circle *T* if the statement is true. Circle *F* if the statement is false.

1. There are mountains on this island.
2. There is a desert in the middle of this island.
3. There is a large bay for ships.
4. There is a forest on this island.
5. There are two rivers.
6. There is a lake.
7. The lake is between the mountains.
8. There is a volcano.
9. The volcano is in the middle of the island.

Energy, Pollution, and Natural Disasters *page 171*

F. Listen to each news report. Write the natural disaster you hear.

1. The Red River is continuing to rise. There are now floods in four cities along the river.
2. There is a hurricane warning for areas along the coast. The hurricane will arrive tomorrow around noon.
3. It is still snowing in the North. The blizzard will leave two to three feet of snow.
4. This is day one hundred of the drought. One hundred days with no rain. And there is no rain in the forecast.
5. Forest fires are burning in four states. Hundreds of firefighters are fighting the fires.
6. We have a report of an avalanche on White Top Mountain.

The United States and Canada *page 173*

E. Listen and write the name of the state you hear.

1. Alaska is the largest state in the United States.
2. Rhode Island is the smallest state in the United States.
3. Florida is called the Sunshine State.
4. Hawaii has many beautiful beaches.
5. California has the highest population in the United States.
6. There are many high mountains in Colorado.
7. Delaware was the first state in the United States.
8. Kansas has many farms.

The World *page 175*

E. Listen. Write the names of the correct countries.

Eleven countries in the world have a population of 100,000,000 people or more.

1. The country with the largest population is China. The population of China is about 1,350,000,000.
2. The population of India is 1,250,000,000.
3. The population of the United States is about 315,000,000.
4. The population of Indonesia is about 243,000,000.
5. The population of Brazil is about 199,000,000.
6. The population of Pakistan is about 190,000,000.
7. The population of Nigeria is about 165,000,000.
8. The population of Bangladesh is about 159,000,000.

The Universe *page 177*

D. Listen to each fact about the planets. Write the name of the correct planet.

1. Jupiter is the largest planet. It is three hundred times larger than Earth.
2. Saturn is famous for its rings. Saturn has thousands of rings made up of ice and rocks.
3. Uranus is a planet of gases. In a telescope, Uranus looks blue.
4. Of course, the Earth is the most beautiful planet. From space, the Earth is blue, white, and green.
5. Sometimes Mars is called "The Red Planet". It is easy to see Mars because it is the closest planet to the Earth.
6. Venus is a small, rocky planet. It has many volcanoes.
7. Mercury is the smallest planet and it is the planet closest to the sun. Because Mercury is close to the sun, it is very hot.

Unit 13: Animals, Plants, and Habitats

Garden *page 179*

E. Listen to each sentence. Circle the flower you hear.

1. Marigolds are easy to grow.
2. Roses are difficult to grow.
3. Plant poppies in the summer.
4. Irises need a lot of water.
5. Daffodils come up in the spring.
6. Chrysanthemums like cool weather.
7. Plant tulips in the fall.

Desert *page 181*

D. Listen to each animal fact. Write the animal you hear.

1. A tortoise can live 100 years or more.
2. A scorpion is an insect with a long tail.
3. A mountain lion lives alone. It does not live in a group or a family.
4. Most insects have six legs, but spiders have eight legs.
5. A desert rat sleeps all day and comes out at night.
6. A lizard likes to rest on rocks.
7. A grasshopper has strong back legs. It can jump far.
8. A camel can walk for many days without water.

Rain Forest *page 183*

D. Where do these animals live? Listen and match the animal and the country or continent.

1. Aardvarks live in Africa.
2. Alligators live in Florida, a state in the United States. They also live in China, in the Yangtze River.
3. Crocodiles live in Australia and in several countries in Southeast Asia.
4. You can find frogs in every country of the world.
5. Orangutans live in Sumatra and in Borneo.
6. You can find panthers in North America and South America.
7. You can see peacocks in India and Sri Lanka.
8. Tigers live in India, China, Indonesia, and Siberia.

Grasslands *page 185*

D. Listen to two children talk about their trip to the zoo. Write the number of each statement under the correct animal.

1. Mom, we saw so many animals at the zoo! First, we saw the kangaroos. They were jumping.
2. And then, we saw the hyenas. The hyenas are really loud. They make a lot of noise.
3. And then we saw the ostriches. Ostriches can't fly.
4. We saw the koalas, too. They're small!
5. And we saw the giraffes. They're so tall and they have really long necks.
6. And then we saw the lions. They were just sleeping.
7. The cheetahs were next to the lions. They were playing with each other.
8. And we saw the elephants. They were so big. They were drinking water.

Polar Lands *page 187*

D. Listen to each animal fact. Write the number of the statement under the correct picture.

1. A wolf lives in a family group with about twenty other wolves.
2. A seal can stay under the water for thirty minutes.
3. A goose lives in the Arctic in the summer. It flies south in the winter.
4. A whale is the largest animal in the world.
5. A falcon has very good eyes. It can see a small animal easily.
6. Polar bears can walk forty miles a day looking for food.
7. A penguin is a bird, but it cannot fly.
8. A male moose has antlers. A female moose does not have antlers.

Sea
page 189

D. Listen to the information about the length of these sea animals. Complete the chart below.

Some animals in the sea are very large. These are some of the larger sea animals.

1. The stingray is about seven feet long.
2. The dolphin is also about eight feet long.
3. The giant octopus is about 15 feet long.
4. The swordfish is about 16 feet long.
5. The white shark is about 23 feet long.
6. The killer whale is about 30 feet long
7. The giant squid is about 60 feet long.

Woodlands
page 191

D. Listen to each speaker. Circle the animal you hear.

1. Look at that beautiful eagle!
2. The robin is looking for a worm.
3. A blue jay is making a nest in the tree.
4. Whew! I smell a skunk.
5. We have deer near our house. They eat everyone's flowers.
6. Listen! Do you hear the woodpecker?
7. Turkeys are large birds. They cannot fly well.

Unit 14: School Subjects

Math
page 193

F. Listen and complete each math problem. Then solve the problem.

a. ten plus five
b. three multiplied by three
c. eight minus five
d. ten divided by five
e. six plus seven
f. twelve minus five
g. eight divided by two
h. ten times five
i. twenty minus five
j. ten plus five plus two

Science
page 195

D. Listen to these science lab instructions. Complete the sentences.

1. Light the Bunsen burner.
2. Clean the slide.
3. Cover the petri dish.
4. Hold the prism in the sunlight.
5. Hand me the forceps.
6. Count the atoms you see.
7. Remove some liquid with the dropper.
8. Fill the test tube with the blue liquid.

Writing
page 197

F. Listen and write the punctuation mark you hear.

1. an exclamation point
2. a comma
3. a question mark
4. a hyphen
5. a period
6. quotation marks
7. parentheses
8. an apostrophe

Explore, Rule, Invent
page 199

D. Listen and complete the sentences.

a. 1850 Elisha Otis invented the modern elevator.
b. 1927 Charles Lindbergh flew across the Atlantic.
c. 1937 The Golden Gate Bridge opened over San Francisco Bay.
d. 1953 Hillary and Norgay reached the top of Mount Everest.
e. 1955 Jonas Salk discovered the polio vaccine.
f. 1975 The Vietnam War ended.
g. 1979 Mother Teresa won the Nobel Peace Prize.
h. 1981 IBM introduced the first personal computer.
i. 1986–94 Workers built a tunnel between England and France.
j. 1994 Kodak introduced the first digital camera for consumers.

U.S. Government and Citizenship
page 201

D. Listen and circle the correct branch of government for each person or place.

1. a congressman
2. the vice president
3. the justices
4. the president
5. a senator
6. the Supreme Court
7. the White House
8. the Capitol

Unit 15: The Arts

Fine Arts
page 203

E. Listen to each statement. Write the number of the statement under the correct picture.

1. This is a portrait of a man.
2. I like that still life.
3. That's a beautiful landscape of the ocean.
4. There's a large mural on that building.
5. Many artists make sketches before they paint.
6. This is a photograph of my great-grandmother.

Performing Arts *page 205*

D. Listen to each speaker. Check the kind(s) of performance(s) each speaker enjoys.

1. I like ballet. I go to the ballet four times a year.
2. I like rock concerts. There are two or three groups I really like, and when they are playing in this area, I go to see them.
3. I live in the city. I love plays. I go to one play a month. And I like the opera. Tickets to the opera are expensive, so I only go one or two times a year.
4. I like plays and rock concerts. I go to a big university and there's a play every month. And rock concerts are great. When there is a concert in this area, I go to it.

Instruments *page 207*

D. Listen and circle the instrument you hear.

1. [guitar]
2. [clarinet]
3. [saxophone]
4. [harp]
5. [piano]
6. [violin]
7. [trumpet]
8. [bass]
9. [drums]
10. [flute]

Film, TV, and Music *page 209*

D. Listen and circle the kind of music you hear.

1. [pop]
2. [rock]
3. [country and western]
4. [soul]
5. [classical]
6. [hip hop]
7. [jazz]

Unit 16: Recreation

The Beach *page 211*

E. Look at the picture of the beach in your dictionary. Listen to each question and circle the correct answer.

1. Where is the shovel?
2. What is the sailboarder wearing?
3. Who is reading a book?
4. How many ships are in the ocean?
5. Where are the sodas?
6. Where is the mask?
7. What is the snorkeler wearing?
8. What color is the lighthouse?
9. Where is the shell?
10. Who is on the pier?

Camping *page 213*

D. Listen to the campers prepare for a camping trip. Write the number of the conversation under the correct item.

1. A: Do you have a sleeping bag?
   B: Yes, I have a sleeping bag.
2. A: And the lantern?
   B: Yes, I bought a new lantern.
3. A: Do you have the camping stove?
   B: No, the camping stove is too heavy.
4. A: Do you have the binoculars?
   B: I can't find the binoculars.
5. A: How about the canteen?
   B: Yes, I have the canteen.
6. A: Do you have the compass?
   B: Yes, I have the compass.
7. A: Do you have your pocket knife?
   B: Yes, it's in my pocket.
8. A: And the tent?
   B: Of course I have the tent!

City Park *page 215*

D. Listen to a mother describe the park in her area. Check the things in the park.

We have a small park in our area. I like to take the children there in the warm weather. It has a nice playground with swings and three slides. My son loves to climb on the jungle gym. And my daughter likes to play in the sandbox. In the summer, the carousel is open. There's a picnic area next to the playground with picnic tables. And there's a path around the park.

Places to Visit *page 217*

D. Listen to each speaker. Where is each person?

1. Win a teddy bear! Throw the ball and knock down three bottles.
2. These flowers are beautiful.
3. Yes! It's a goal! The score is now three - one.
4. Look! You can see the moon and the stars and the planets.
5. Dad, look at the elephants!
6. Let's buy this lamp. It's only three dollars.
7. Are you ready to order lunch?

Indoor Sports and Fitness *page 219*

D. Listen to each speaker. What sport or activity does each person enjoy at the gym?

1. I like the stationary bike. I watch TV while I use the bike.
2. I take a yoga class.
3. I use the treadmill before work. I walk on the treadmill and listen to music.
4. I take a fitness class three days a week.
5. I play ping-pong. I'm the best at our club.
6. I enjoy weightlifting. I can lift 100 pounds.
7. I do martial arts twice a week.

Outdoor Sports and Fitness *page 221*

E. Listen to the sports reporter. Write the name of the correct sport.

1. The score is 7 to 10. Greta has the ball. . . .She serves. . . . She hits it into the net.
2. Roger swings. And . . . it's a home run!
3. We are here, at the Glendale Golf Course. The players are at the fourth hole. It's a par 3.
4. Great serve! The score is thirty-love.
5. It's Martinez. Garcia. Romero. He passes to Vargas. And . . . goal! It's a goal! Mexico leads 2 to 1.
6. The football is on the 30-yard line. The quarterback has the ball. . . . He throws it to Jasper . . . Incomplete.

Winter Sports *page 223*

D. Listen and write the number of each conversation under the correct picture.

1. A: Dad, can you take us to the park?
   B: Yeah! We want to use our new sled.
2. A: Are you ready to go skiing?
   B: I can't find my ski poles.
   A: I put them in the car.
3. A: Mom, I need new ski boots.
   B: What's the problem?
   A: These boots are too small.
4. A: We need to stop at the gas station.
   B: Why?
   A: We need gas for the snowmobile.
5. A: Have you ever used snowshoes?
   B: No.
   A: I have. They're fun!
6. A: Do you want to go ice skating?
   B: Sure.
   A: Get your ice skates and we can go now.

Games, Toys, and Hobbies *page 225*

D. Listen and complete.

1. king of diamonds
2. queen of hearts
3. ace of spades
4. queen of spades
5. jack of clubs
6. king of spades
7. ace of diamonds
8. jack of hearts
9. queen of clubs

Camera, Stereo, and DVD *page 227*

D. What equipment would each person like? Write the number of each statement with the correct item.

1. We have a new baby. I'd like a camcorder to take some movies of him to send to my parents.
2. We don't get good reception. I'd like to put a satellite dish on the roof.
3. I'd like a boom box to take to the beach in the summer.
4. My mom says my music is too loud. I'd like some headphones.
5. I'm taking a photography course. I'd like a 35-millimeter camera.
6. I love music. I'd like a nice stereo system in the house.
7. My children would like a video game system.

Holidays and Celebrations *page 229*

C. Listen to each statement or song. Which holiday or event are the people celebrating?

1. To thank you for your many years of service to the company, we would like to give you this gold watch.
2. [Happy Birthday song]
3. [We Wish You a Merry Christmas song]
4. Happy New Year!
5. I love you, sweetheart.
6. This turkey is delicious.
7. Happy Mother's Day!
8. Look at you! You're a princess! And you're a scary monster! Here's some candy.